Bond
No.1 for exam success

Maths

Assessment Papers

10-11+ years

Book 1

OXFORD
UNIVERSITY PRESS

Great Clarendon Street, Oxford, OX2 6DP, United Kingdom

Oxford University Press is a department of the University of Oxford.
It furthers the University's objective of excellence in research, scholarship,
and education by publishing worldwide. Oxford is a registered trade mark of
Oxford University Press in the UK and in certain other countries

British Library Cataloguing in Publication Data
Data available

978-0-19-277641-9

10 9 8 7 6 5 4 3 2 1

Paper used in the production of this book is a natural, recyclable
product made from wood grown in sustainable forests.
The manufacturing process conforms to the environmental
regulations of the country of origin.

Printed in China

Acknowledgements

The publishers would like to thank the following for permissions to
use copyright material:

Page make-up: OKS Prepress, India
Illustrations: Tech-Set Limited
Cover illustrations: Lo Cole

Although we have made every effort to trace and contact all
copyright holders before publication this has not been possible in all
cases. If notified, the publisher will rectify any errors or omissions at
the earliest opportunity.

The publisher would like to thank Michellejoy Hughes for assisting
with the compilation of the expanded answers.

Links to third party websites are provided by Oxford in good faith
and for information only. Oxford disclaims any responsibility for
the materials contained in any third party website referenced in
this work.

Before you get started

What is Bond?

This book is part of the Bond Assessment Papers series for maths, which provides **thorough and continuous practice of all the key maths content** from ages five to thirteen. Bond's maths resources are ideal preparation for many different kinds of tests and exams – from SATs to 11+ and other secondary school selection exams.

How does the scope of this book match real exam content?

Maths 10–11+ Book 1 and Book 2 are the core Bond 11+ books. Each paper is **pitched at the level of a typical 11+ exam** and covers the key maths a child would be expected to learn. The papers are also in line with other selective exams for this age group. The coverage is matched to the National Curriculum and the National Numeracy Strategy and will also **provide invaluable preparation for Key Stage 2 SATs**. One of the key features of Bond Assessment Papers is that each one practises **a wide variety of skills and question types** so that children are always challenged to think – and don't get bored repeating the same question type again and again. We think that variety is the key to effective learning. It helps children 'think on their feet' and cope with the unexpected.

What does the book contain?

- **24 papers** – each one contains 50 questions.

- **Tutorial links throughout** – B 7 – this icon appears in the margin next to the questions. It indicates links to the relevant section in *How to do … 11+ Maths*, our invaluable subject guide that offers explanations and practice for all core question types.

- **Scoring devices** – there are score boxes in the margins and a Progress Chart on page 64. The chart is a visual and motivating way for children to see how they are doing. It also turns the score into a percentage that can help decide what to do next.

- **Next Steps Planner** – advice on what to do after finishing the papers can be found on the inside back cover.

- **Answers** – located in an easily-removed central pull-out section.

How can you use this book?

One of the great strengths of Bond Assessment Papers is their flexibility. They can be used at home, in school and by tutors to:

- set **timed formal practice** tests – allow about 30 minutes per paper in line with standard 11+ demands. Reduce the suggested time limit by five minutes to practise working at speed.

- provide **bite-sized chunks** for regular practice.

- **highlight strengths and weaknesses** in the core skills.

- identify **individual needs**.

- set **homework**.

- follow **a complete 11+ preparation strategy** alongside *The Parents' Guide to the 11+* (see below).

It is best to start at the beginning and work through the papers in order. Calculators should not be used. Remind children to check whether each answer needs a unit of measurement before they start a test. If units of measurement are not included in answers that require them, they will lose marks for those questions. To ensure that children can practise including them in their answers, units of measurement have been omitted after the answer rules for some questions. If you are using the book as part of a careful run-in to the 11+, we suggest that you also have two other essential Bond resources close at hand:

How to do … 11+ Maths: the subject guide that explains all the question types practised in this book. Use the cross-reference icons to find the relevant sections.

The Parents' Guide to the 11+: the step-by-step guide to the whole 11+ experience. It clearly explains the 11+ process, provides guidance on how to assess children, helps you to set complete action plans for practice and explains how you can use the *Maths 10-11+ Book 1 and Book 2* as part of a strategic run-in to the exam.

See the inside front cover for more details of these books.

What does a score mean and how can it be improved?

It is unfortunately impossible to guarantee that a child will pass the 11+ exam if they achieve a certain score on any practice book or paper. Success on the day depends on a host of factors, including the scores of the other children sitting the test. However, we can give some guidance on what a score indicates and how to improve it.

If children colour in the Progress Chart on page 64, this will give an idea of present performance in percentage terms. The Next Steps Planner inside the back cover will help you to decide what to do next to help a child progress. It is always valuable to go over wrong answers with children. If they are having trouble with any particular question type, follow the tutorial links to *How to do … 11+ Maths* for step-by-step explanations and further practice.

Don't forget the website …!

Visit www.bond11plus.co.uk for lots of advice, information and suggestions on everything to do with Bond, the 11+ and helping children to do their best.

Key words

Some special maths words are used in this book. You will find them **in bold** each time they appear in the papers. These words are explained here.

acute angle   an angle that is less than a right angle

coordinates   the two numbers, the first horizontal the second vertical, that plot a point on a grid, for example (3, 2)

factor   the factors of a number are numbers that divide into it, for example 1, 2, 4 and 8 are all factors of 8

kite   a four-sided shape that looks like a stretched diamond

lowest term   the simplest you can make a fraction, for example $\frac{4}{10}$ reduced to the lowest term is $\frac{2}{5}$

mean   one kind of average. You find the mean by adding all the scores together and dividing by the number of scores, for example the mean of 1, 3 and 8 is 4

median   one kind of average, the middle number of a set of numbers after being ordered from lowest to highest, for example the median of 1, 3 and 8 is 3 for example the median of 7, 4, 6 and 9 is 6.5 (halfway between 6 and 7)

mixed number   a number that contains a whole number and a fraction, for example $5\frac{1}{2}$ is a mixed number

mode   one kind of average. The most common number in a set of numbers, for example the mode of 2, 3, 2, 7, 2 is 2

obtuse angle   an angle that is more than 90° and not more than 180°

parallelogram   a four-sided shape that has all its opposite sides equal and parallel

polygon   a closed shape with many sides

prime factor   the factors of a number that are also prime numbers, for example the prime factors of 12 are 2 and 3

prime number   any number that can only be divided by itself or 1. 2, 3, 5 and 7 are prime numbers. (Note that 1 is not a prime number.)

quotient   the answer if you divide one number by another, for example the quotient of 12 ÷ 4 is 3

range   the difference between the largest and smallest of a set of numbers, for example the range of 1, 2, 5, 3, 6, 8 is 7

reflex angle   an angle that is bigger than 180°

rhombus   a four-sided shape, like a squashed square, that has all its sides of equal length and its opposite sides parallel

trapezium   a four-sided shape that has just one pair of parallel sides

vertex, vertices   the point where two or more edges or sides in a shape meet

Paper 1

1–5 Here is a pie chart which shows how Joanna spent yesterday evening between 6 p.m. and 8 p.m.

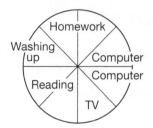

Joanna was watching TV for _____ min, doing homework for _____ min, reading for _____ min, washing up for _____ min and was on the computer for _____ min.

6–8 What is the average (**mean**) of the following numbers?

7 4 6 8 5 _____   3 2 7 _____   4 4 6 2 _____

9 Make 999 ten times as large.   _____

In each of the following lines, underline the smallest number and put a ring round the largest number.

10–11 $\frac{5}{8}$ $\frac{3}{4}$ $\frac{7}{8}$ $\frac{6}{8}$ $\frac{1}{2}$

12–13 3.07   3.7   37   3.007   0.307

14–15 $\frac{15}{3}$ $\frac{12}{6}$ $\frac{27}{9}$ $\frac{8}{2}$ $\frac{10}{10}$

16–17 0.125 $\frac{1}{2}$ 0.25 $\frac{7}{8}$ 0.75

18–19 $\frac{3}{4}$ of 12 $\frac{5}{7}$ of 14 $\frac{2}{3}$ of 9 $\frac{2}{5}$ of 10 $\frac{1}{2}$ of 16

20 Write in figures: one hundred and two thousand and twenty-one.   _____

21–24

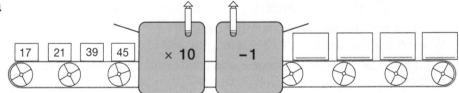

What is the size of the smaller angle:

25 between 1 and 3?   _____

26 between 2 and 7?   _____

27 between 7 and 11?   _____

 B 14
 B 3
 5
 B 15
 3
 B 1
 1
 B 10
B 11
10
B 1
1
 B 9
 4
 B 17
3

28–29 John used this decision tree to sort paint. What is missing from the tree? Fill in the gaps.

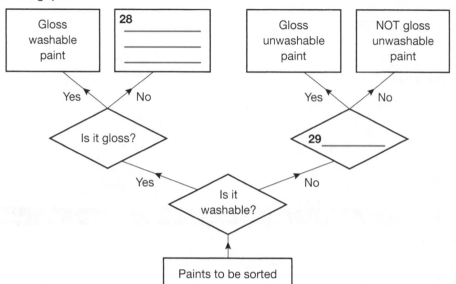

2

Complete these calculations.

B3/B2

30 $(7 \times 8) +$ _____ $= 61$ **31** $(9 \times 12) -$ _____ $= 106$

32 $8 \times (7 -$ _____$) = 32$ **33** $6 \times (11 -$ _____$) = 36$

4

34–37 Plot the points (3, 5), (−1, 5), (3, −2) on the grid.

These points are the **vertices** of a rectangle. Mark the fourth **vertex** and draw the rectangle.

38 The **coordinates** of the fourth **vertex** are (_____ , _____).

B 23

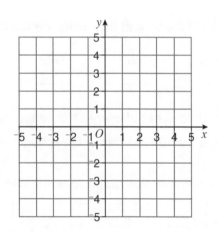

5

Write the times which are a quarter of an hour before the following.

B 27

39 22:00 _____   **40** 11:05 _____   **41** 13:10 _____

B 10

3

Thirty-six articles are shared among A, B and C in the ratio of 1 : 3 : 5. How many articles does each person have?

B 13

42 A has _____   **43** B has _____   **44** C has _____

3

Put a sign in each space to make these calculations correct.

45 45 _____ 7 = 52   **46** 33 _____ 3 = 11

47 678 _____ 56 = 37 968   **48** 90 _____ 5 = 18

49 What is the area of this shape?   _____ cm²

50 What is the perimeter of this shape?   _____ cm

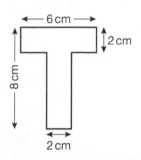

6 cm

2 cm

8 cm

2 cm

Now go to the Progress Chart to record your score!   Total   50

Paper 2

Divide each of these numbers by 10.

1 78.65 _____   **2** 6.54 _____

3 467.5 _____   **4** 0.123 _____

5–8 Work out these, and then write them out in order, from highest to lowest **quotient**.

7)315   8)392   7)329   9)387

_____   _____   _____   _____

9–10 In a school 6 out of every 11 children are girls.

If there are 407 children in the school there are: _____ boys and _____ girls.

11–12 Use the conversion graph to rewrite the road sign in kilometres.

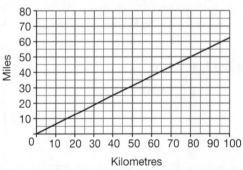

| Darlington | 25 miles |
| Newcastle | 50 miles |

| Darlington | _____ km |
| Newcastle | _____ km |

13 Approximately how many miles in 95 km?   _____

14 Which is greater: 50 miles or 75 km?   _____

Put a sign in each space to make these calculations correct.

15 74 _____ 5 = 14.8   **16** 74 _____ 5 = 79

17 74 _____ 5 = 69   **18** 74 _____ 5 = 370

4

There are six balls, numbered 1 to 6, in a bag.   B 16

19 What is the probability that I will draw out an even-numbered ball? _____

20 What is the probability that I will draw out the 5? _____

21 What is the probability that I will draw out an odd-numbered ball? _____   3

22-24 Put a circle around each **prime number**.   B 6

3   4   5   6   7   3

B 2

25 What number is midway between 18 and 42? _____

26 What number is midway between 19 and 53? _____   2

27 Find the area of a square whose perimeter is 12 cm. _____   B 20

1

Using this world time chart answer the following.   B 27

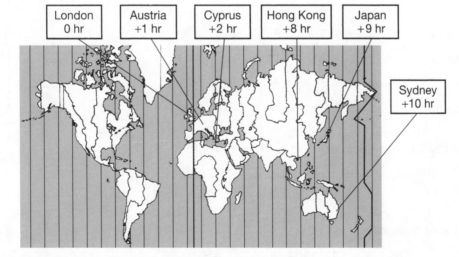

| London 0 hr | Austria +1 hr | Cyprus +2 hr | Hong Kong +8 hr | Japan +9 hr |

Sydney +10 hr

3

Using a 24 hour clock, when it is midday in Japan it is:

28 _____ in London.   **29** _____ in Hong Kong.

30 It is 12:00 midday in Cyprus. Using a 24 hour clock, what time is it in Austria? _____

31 It is 4:36 p.m. in Hong Kong. What time is it in London? _____   4

A fair coin is tossed at the start of a game. Underline the correct answer to each question.

32 What is the probability of getting a head?

$\frac{2}{3}$ $\quad$ $\frac{4}{5}$ $\quad$ $\frac{1}{2}$ $\quad$ $\frac{3}{4}$

33 What is the probability of getting a tail?

$\frac{2}{3}$ $\quad$ $\frac{4}{5}$ $\quad$ $\frac{1}{2}$ $\quad$ $\frac{3}{4}$

Which numbers are the arrows pointing to on this number line?

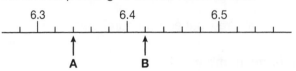

34 Arrow A points to _____

35 Arrow B points to _____

36 $\frac{5}{8} + \frac{7}{16} =$ _____

37 $7 - 4\frac{2}{9} =$ _____

Some game cards are shared between Thomas and Matthew in the ratio of 5 : 4.

38 If Matthew receives 16 Thomas will get _____ .

39 If they shared the same cards equally (not in 5 : 4) Matthew would receive _____ .

40 The **median** of $\quad$ 1 $\quad$ 3 $\quad$ 8 $\quad$ is $\quad$ _____

41 The **median** of $\quad$ 20 $\quad$ 34 $\quad$ 11 $\quad$ is $\quad$ _____

42 The **median** of $\quad$ 4 $\quad$ 3 $\quad$ 3 $\quad$ is $\quad$ _____

43 The **median** of $\quad$ 5 $\quad$ 9 $\quad$ 3 $\quad$ 7 $\quad$ is $\quad$ _____

44–46 Write these fractions as decimals.

$4\frac{1}{2}$ $\quad$ $7\frac{1}{10}$ $\quad$ $3\frac{9}{100}$ $\qquad$ _____ $\quad$ _____ $\quad$ _____

47–50 Complete these questions.

$$
\begin{array}{cccc}
887 & 378 & 12\overline{)2808} & 456 \\
998 & \times\ 9 & & \times\ 35 \\
+\ 776 & & & \\
\end{array}
$$

_____ $\qquad$ _____ $\qquad\qquad$ _____

Now go to the Progress Chart to record your score! $\quad$ Total $\quad$ **50**

B 16
B 10
2
B 26
2
B 10
2
B 13
2
B 15
4
B10 B11
3
B2 B3
4

Paper 3

1 Which of the numbers in the oval is 2^2? _____

2 Which of the numbers in the oval is 5^2? _____

3 Which of the numbers in the oval is 3^2 _____

4 Which of the numbers in the oval is 6^2 _____

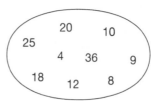

B 6

4

5–15 Complete this timetable for Merrywell School. There are five lessons each 35 minutes in length, with a break of 15 minutes after the third lesson.

	Begins	Ends
1st lesson	_____	_____
2nd lesson	_____	_____
3rd lesson	_____	_____
Break	_____	1:10
4th lesson	_____	_____
5th lesson	_____	_____

B 27

11

16 What is the nearest number to 1000, but smaller than 1000, into which 38 will divide with no remainder? _____

B3 B5

1

What is the area of:

17 side A? _____   18 side B? _____

19 side C? _____

What is the perimeter of:

20 side A? _____   21 side B? _____

22 side C? _____

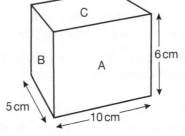

B 20

B 20

6

Which number is represented by each symbol?

23 $2 \times \Delta = 4 \times 5$ $\Delta =$ _____

24 $5 \times \clubsuit = 27 - 2$ $\clubsuit =$ _____

25 $\otimes \times 3 = 36 \div 3$ $\otimes =$ _____

26 $\blacklozenge \times 4 = 10 + 10$ $\blacklozenge =$ _____

B8 B3

B 2

4

Chris is 11 years old and Emma is 9.
They are given £40 to be shared between them in the ratio of their ages.

27 Chris will get _____   **28** Emma will get _____

29 If 11 items cost £7.37, what would be the cost of 8 items? _____

Find the area of these triangles.

Scale: 1 square = 1 cm²

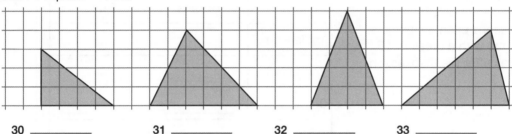

30 _____   **31** _____   **32** _____   **33** _____

At our car park the charges are as follows:

Up to 1 hour   £1.00
Over 1 hour and up to 2 hours   £1.75
Over 2 hours and up to 4 hours   £3.50
Over 4 hours and up to 6 hours   £5.25
Over 6 hours and up to 8 hours   £7.00

34 Miss Short parks her car at 12:30 p.m. and collects it at 4 p.m.
How much will she have to pay? _____

35 Mrs Patel parks her car at 9:15 a.m. and collects it at 11:30 a.m.
How much will she have to pay? _____

36 Mr Samuels parks his car at 2:20 p.m. and collects it at 6:30 p.m.
How much will he have to pay? _____

37 Mr Davies parks his car at 8:45 a.m. and collects it at 4:30 p.m.
How much will he have to pay? _____

38–43 VAT (Value Added Tax) is charged at 20% on some goods.
This means that a £100.00 article would have a tax of £20 added to its cost.
Complete the table below.

Price before VAT	VAT	Total cost
£180.00	_____	_____
£420.00	_____	_____
£340.00	_____	_____

44	m	cm		45	m	cm		46	m	cm
	4	72			6	2			4	60
+ 3		39		− 3		8		×		5
		___				___				___

47–50 Write these numbers to the nearest 100.

298   847   503   1074

___   ___   ___   ___

Now go to the Progress Chart to record your score!   Total   ◯ 50

Paper 4

1–5 Fill in the gaps.

	Length	Width	Perimeter
Rectangle 1	18 cm	___	40 cm
Rectangle 2	___	3 cm	30 cm
Rectangle 3	9 cm	4 cm	___
Square	6 cm	___	___

◯ 5

6 How many times can 28 be subtracted from 1316?   ___

B 3
◯ 1

7–12 Circle the correct answer in each line.

0.1×0.1	=	0.2	0.02	0.01	0.1	1.1
10% of 40	=	8	5	80	20	4
$10 - 9.99$	=	0.9	0.01	1.00	1.1	1.9
$0.207 \div 0.3$	=	0.9	0.09	0.69	0.66	0.23
1.1×1.1	=	1.21	1.11	11.1	2.2	1.01
$567 \div 100$	=	56 700	0.567	56.7	5.67	5670

◯ 6

13 The product of two numbers is 1260. One of the numbers is 35.
What is the other number?   ___

B 3
◯ 1

9

14–20 Write the missing digits or answer.

```
   _365            1_7_           345                 38
   2_ _1         -  2_5         ×   _            9)
 + 345_          ------         ------             -----
 ------            786           2415
 10603
```

Find the value of y in the following equations.

21 $3y = 10 - 1$

$y =$ _____

22 $4y - y = 12$

$y =$ _____

23 $2y + y = 6$

$y =$ _____

24 $3y + y = 11 + 1$

$y =$ _____

Which numbers are the arrows pointing to on this number line?

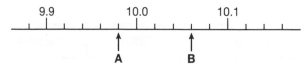

9.9   10.0   10.1

A   B

25 Arrow A points to _____

26 Arrow B points to _____

A fair dice numbered 1 to 6 is rolled at the start of a game. Underline the correct answer to each question.

27 What is the probability of getting a 6?

$\frac{2}{3}$ $\frac{1}{6}$ $\frac{1}{2}$ $\frac{3}{4}$

28 What is the probability of getting a 5?

$\frac{1}{3}$ $\frac{1}{4}$ $\frac{1}{5}$ $\frac{1}{6}$

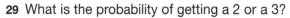

29 What is the probability of getting a 2 or a 3?

$\frac{1}{6}$ $\frac{1}{3}$ $\frac{1}{2}$ $\frac{2}{3}$

What are the missing numbers in these number squares?

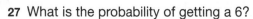

38	34	30
42	38	34
x	42	38

102	120	y
84	102	120
66	84	102

z	27	31
27	31	35
31	35	39

30 $x =$ _____

31 $y =$ _____

32 $z =$ _____

10

Multiply each of these numbers by 10.

B 1

33 3.77 _____ **34** 46.5 _____

35 0.126 _____ **36** 0.027 _____

37 49 _____ **38** 567 _____

39 0.0023 _____

7

Find the **median** of the following sets of numbers.

B 15

40 4 6 8 10 _____

41 8 2 6 8 _____

42 54 21 7 19 _____

43 1 2 3 4 5 6 _____

44 32 21 60 3 5 17 _____

45 45 47 _____

6

Change these 24-hour times into 12-hour times using a.m. or p.m.

B 27

46 05:05 _____ **47** 12:45 _____ **48** 20:02 _____

49 15:15 _____ **50** 11:14 _____

5

Now go to the Progress Chart to record your score!   Total   50

Paper 5

1–7 Complete the following chart.

B 20

	Length	Width	Area
Rectangle 1	8 m	6 m	_____
Rectangle 2	_____	4 m	32 m²
Rectangle 3	4 m	_____	10 m²
Rectangle 4	_____	3.5 m	10.5 m²
Rectangle 5	1.5 m	1.5 m	_____
Rectangle 6	5 m	_____	6 m²
Rectangle 7	1.3 m	2 m	_____

7

Find the area of these triangles.

Scale: 1 square = 1 cm^2

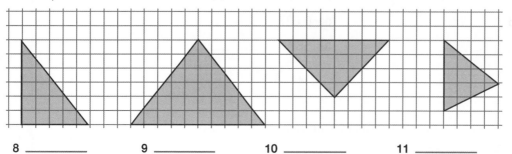

8 _____   9 _____   10 _____   11 _____

12 My watch loses a quarter of a minute every hour. If I put it right at midday, what time will my watch show at 8 p.m. that evening? _____

A class carried out a survey to find the most popular subject.

Favourite subject	Votes
English	5
Mathematics	12
PE	7
Music	6

13 Which is the most popular subject? _____

14 Which is the least popular subject? _____

15 How many votes are there in total? _____

16 What is the **mean** number of votes? _____

17–22 Complete the table.

∇	2	4	6	8	10	12
$2 \times \nabla =$						

Reduce these prices by 10%.

23 £50 _____   24 £110 _____

25 £250 _____   26 £40 _____

27 £30 _____   28 £280 _____

 B 18
 4
 B 27
 1
 B 2
 B 15
 4
 B 3
 6
 B 12
 B 2
 6

29–30 One day 20% of the children were away from school on a visit to a museum.

If there were 360 children altogether, _____ children were in school and _____ were on the museum trip.

B 12

2

31 A number multiplied by itself is 16. What is the number? _____

B 6

1

32 How many US dollars do you get for £10? _____

33 How many Kenyan shillings do you get for £100? _____

34 How many euros do you get for £1000? _____

£1 = 1.46 US dollars
£1 = 119 Kenyan shillings
£1 = 1.16 euros

B 3

B 13

3

A bag contains 4 grey balls and 3 white balls. Underline the correct answer to each question.

B 16

35 What is the probability of picking a white ball?

$\frac{3}{4}$ $\frac{3}{5}$ $\frac{3}{6}$ $\frac{3}{7}$ $\frac{3}{8}$

36 What is the probability of picking a grey ball?

0     $\frac{1}{2}$ $\frac{4}{7}$ $\frac{3}{7}$ $\frac{3}{4}$

37 What is the probability of picking a black ball?

0     $\frac{1}{2}$ $\frac{4}{7}$ $\frac{3}{7}$ $\frac{3}{4}$

3

38 What number when divided by 12, has an answer 11 remainder 5? _____

B 3

1

A show starts at 7:30 p.m. The first half of the programme lasts 1 hour 35 minutes, then there is an interval of 8 minutes.

B 27

39 When does the second half of the show begin? _____ p.m.

1

A rectangular field is 3 times as long as it is wide. If the perimeter is 0.8 km:

B 20

40 what is the length? _____

41 what is the width? _____

42 what is the area? _____

3

43 I have enough tinned dog food to last my 2 dogs for 18 days. If I got another dog, how long would this food last? _____

44 Add the greatest number to the smallest number. _____

565   656   556   655   566   665

45 What number is halfway between 37 and 111? _____

46–47 Put a circle around the **prime numbers**.

12   13   14   15   16   17   18

48–50 What are the **prime factors** of 60? _____ and _____ and _____

8

Now go to the Progress Chart to record your score!   **Total**   50

Paper 6

1–3 Write down the numbers that will come out of this machine.

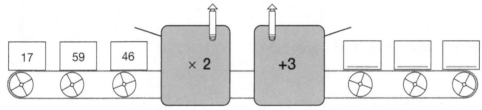

3

4–8 Here are five 'regular **polygons**'.

Give the size of each angle at the centre of these **polygons**.

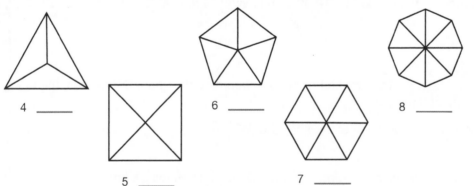

4 _____

5 _____

6 _____

7 _____

8 _____

5

Convert the following lengths to metres.

9 245 cm = _____ m   **10** 1342 cm = _____ m   **11** 12345 cm = _____ m

3

14

Convert the following lengths to kilometres.

12 1357 m = _____ km

13 12 986 m = _____ km

14 456 m = _____ km

B 25

○ 3

15–16 There are 30 children in Class 4. 60% of them are girls.

There are _____ girls and _____ boys.

B 12

○ 2

17 Which number, when multiplied by 30, will give the same answer as 51 × 10? _____

B 3

18 Write the number which is 7 less than 2000. _____

B 2

○ 2

19–34 Insert a sign in each space so that the answer given for each line and column is correct.

B 2
B 3

3		3		2	=	7
	■		■		■	
6		4		5	=	5
	■		■		■	
2		5		4	=	6
=	■	=	■	=	■	=
9		2		6	=	12

○ 16

35 If 9 items cost £6.30, what will be the cost of 11 items? _____

B 3

○ 1

Here is a list of some of the longest rivers in the world.

Write the length of each river to the nearest 1000 km.

B 1

36 Amazon 6516 km _____ km

37 Chang Jiang 6380 km _____ km

38 Nile 6695 km _____ km

39 Paraná 4500 km _____ km

40 Mississippi–Missouri 6019 km _____ km

41 Zaire 4667 km _____ km

○ 6

Fill in the spaces with one of these signs. $<$ $>$ $=$

42 8×9 _____ 6×12

43 $8 + 9 + 7$ _____ $30 - 3$

44 0.5 m _____ 45 cm

45 23 _____ 3^2

46 12^2 _____ 144

47 50 min _____ $\frac{3}{4}$ hour

Consider a fair dice with faces numbered 1 to 6.

What is the probability of rolling:

48 a 4 or a 5? _____   **49** a 7? _____

50 a whole number greater than 0 and less than 7? _____

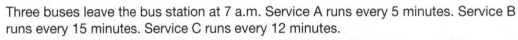

Now go to the Progress Chart to record your score!   **Total** ⬭ **50**

Paper 7

Underline the correct answer in each line.

1 0.2×0.2 $=$ 0.4 4 40 0.04 0.004

2 $\frac{1}{2} + \frac{1}{4}$ $=$ $\frac{2}{6}$ $\frac{3}{4}$ $\frac{2}{4}$ $\frac{2}{8}$ $\frac{1}{8}$

3 50% of 30 $=$ 35 20 25 130 15

4 $10 \div \frac{1}{2}$ $=$ 20 5 $10\frac{1}{2}$ $\frac{1}{20}$ $\frac{1}{5}$

5 $5 \div 0.5$ $=$ 0.1 0.01 100 10 0.001

6 $412 \div 4$ $=$ 13 103 104 12 14

7 $\frac{1}{8} + \frac{1}{2}$ $=$ $\frac{1}{16}$ $\frac{1}{10}$ $\frac{5}{8}$ $\frac{1}{2}$ $\frac{3}{8}$

Three buses leave the bus station at 7 a.m. Service A runs every 5 minutes. Service B runs every 15 minutes. Service C runs every 12 minutes.

8 At what time will all three services again start from the bus station at the same time? _____

Here is a list of some of the highest mountains in the world.
Write the height of each mountain to the nearest 1000 feet.

9 Aconcagua   22 837 feet   ——————— feet

10 Everest   29 029 feet   ——————— feet

11 K2   28 251 feet   ——————— feet

12 Kilimanjaro   19 336 feet   ——————— feet

13 McKinley   20 320 feet   ——————— feet

14 Mont Blanc   15 782 feet   ——————— feet   6

15 What number, when multiplied by 10, has the same answer as 15 × 12?   ——   B 3

1

16–18 Andrew has half as many apps as Stuart, who has half as many as Meena.   B 13
      Together they have 140 apps.

      Meena has ——— apps, Stuart has ——— and Andrew has ——— .   3

Here is the attendance record of 40 children for one week of the term.   B 15

Attendance	Mon	Tues	Wed	Thurs	Fri
Morning	36	33	37	34	35
Afternoon	39	36	38	36	36

19 What was the **mean** (average) morning attendance?   ——————

20 What was the **median** afternoon attendance?   ——————

21 What was the **mode** afternoon attendance?   ——————   3

Multiply each of these numbers by 1000.   B 1

22 37.8 ——————   23 2.45 ——————

24 0.047 ——————   25 25.0 ——————

26 0.82 ——————   5

27 $7\frac{7}{8} + 5\frac{13}{16} =$ ——————   B 10

28 $7\frac{1}{5} - 3\frac{11}{15} =$ ——————   2

29 What is the total area of the flag? _____

30 What is the area of the cross? _____

31 What is the area of the grey area? _____

32 What is the perimeter of the flag? _____

33 What is the perimeter of the cross? _____

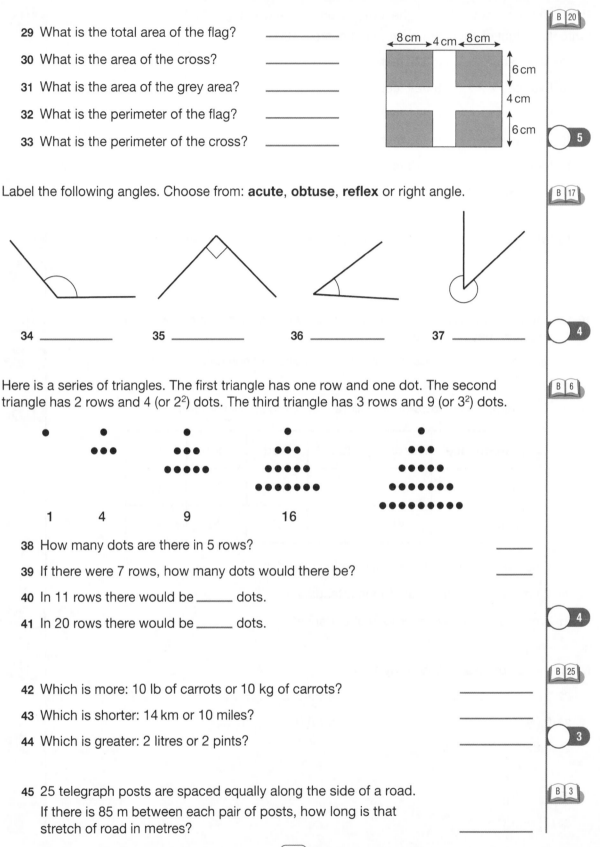

Label the following angles. Choose from: **acute**, **obtuse**, **reflex** or right angle.

34 _____ **35** _____ **36** _____ **37** _____

Here is a series of triangles. The first triangle has one row and one dot. The second triangle has 2 rows and 4 (or 2^2) dots. The third triangle has 3 rows and 9 (or 3^2) dots.

1   4   9   16

38 How many dots are there in 5 rows? _____

39 If there were 7 rows, how many dots would there be? _____

40 In 11 rows there would be _____ dots.

41 In 20 rows there would be _____ dots.

42 Which is more: 10 lb of carrots or 10 kg of carrots? _____

43 Which is shorter: 14 km or 10 miles? _____

44 Which is greater: 2 litres or 2 pints? _____

45 25 telegraph posts are spaced equally along the side of a road. If there is 85 m between each pair of posts, how long is that stretch of road in metres? _____

46 A man's salary was £36000. He is given a 5% increase.
What is his new salary? _____

47 A cricketer's average score for 6 innings is 12 runs.
What must he score in his next innings to make his average 13? _____

48 Add together 4.5 m, 16.7 m and 127.09 m. _____

4

49–50 Complete the drawings below using the line of symmetry marked by the dashes.

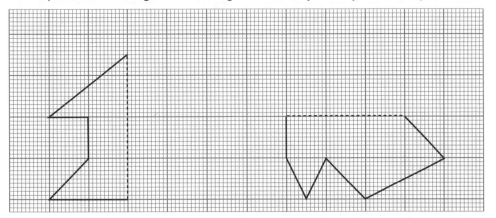

2

Now go to the Progress Chart to record your score! **Total** **50**

Paper 8

1 What is the difference between 0.225 tonnes and 128 kg? _____ kg

2 If $a = 2$ and $b = 3$, find the value of $4a - 2b$. _____

3 A book has 38 lines to each page.
On which page will the 1000th line appear? _____

3

Change these 12-hour times into 24-hour times.

4 10:10 a.m. _____

5 11:20 p.m. _____

6 1:01 a.m. _____

7 7:45 p.m. _____

4

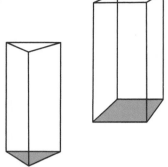

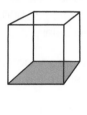

Name of solid	Number of faces	Number of vertices	Number of edges
Triangular prism			
Square prism			
Triangular-based pyramid			
Square-based pyramid			
Cube			

15

23 Mrs Forgetmenot is 9 minutes late for the 9.42 a.m. train.
How long will she have to wait for the train at 10.27 a.m.? _____

1

24–28 Local clubs took part in a 'clean the beach' campaign. Work out the percentage of members from each club that took part in this activity.

Club	Number of members	Number who took part	Percentage
A	100	79	_____
B	50	36	_____
C	150	120	_____
D	70	49	_____
E	80	60	_____

5

29 If $x = 5$ and $y = 2$ then $\dfrac{4x}{5y} =$ _____

1

30–40 Complete the timetable for Workmore School. There are five lessons, each 30 minutes long, with a break of 15 minutes after the third lesson.

	Begins	**Ends**
1st lesson	_____	_____
2nd lesson	_____	_____
3rd lesson	_____	_____
Break	_____	_____
4th lesson	_____	_____
5th lesson	_____	12:25

41 Three whole numbers multiplied together total 2475. Two of the numbers are 25 and 11. What is the third number? _____

42–43 5 is a **prime factor** of 2475.
What are the other two prime factors? _____ and _____

£1 = 10.75 Norwegian krone	£1 = 8.54 Danish krone
£1 = 1.15 euros	£1 = 1.72 Australian dollars

44 How many Norwegian krone do you get for £3? _____ Norwegian krone

45 How many Danish krone do you get for £1.50? _____ Danish krone

46 How many euros do you get for £13? _____ euros

47 How many Australian dollars do you get for £50? _____ Australian dollars

There are 351 children in a school. There are 7 boys to every 6 girls.

48 How many boys are there? _____

49 How many girls are there? _____

A number multiplied by itself and then doubled is 242.

50 What is the number? _____

11

10

B5 B6

3

B3/B13

4

2

B3/B13

1

Now go to the Progress Chart to record your score! **Total** 50

Paper 9

Use these words to help you name the following shapes:
rhombus, **kite**, **parallelogram**, **trapezium**, rectangle.

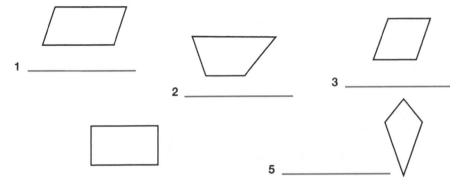

1 _____

2 _____

3 _____

4 _____

5 _____

On one day in February the temperatures in different places were:

| Chicago | −3 °C | Montreal | −10 °C | Singapore | 31 °C |
| Cape Town | 27 °C | Miami | 26 °C | Toronto | −5 °C |

6 Which was the hottest of these places?   _____

7 Which was the coldest?   _____

8 How much colder was it in Chicago than Cape Town?   _____

9 The difference between Toronto and Miami was   _____

10 The difference between Singapore and Montreal was   _____

11 Form the largest number possible with the digits 3, 9, 7 and 2 and then
    take away the smallest possible number. What is your answer?   _____

12 How many comics, costing £1.75 each, can be bought for £15.00?   _____

13 In a certain question Mia multiplied by 7 instead of dividing by 7.
    Her answer was 6027. What should it have been?

$y \times 7 = 6027$ ✗ $y \div 7 =$ _____ ✓

Write the next two numbers in each line.

14–15 $3\frac{1}{2}$ $4\frac{1}{4}$ 5 $5\frac{3}{4}$ _____ _____

16–17 100 90 81 73 _____ _____

18–19 47 52 58 65 _____ _____

20–21 2 5 11 20 _____ _____

22–23 2 4 8 16 _____ _____

5

5

10

24–25 The perimeter of a rectangular piece of paper is 48 cm.
The length is 3 times the width. The length is _____ and the width is _____

26–30

NW N NE
W —— E
SW S SE

You start facing	turn through	clockwise/ anticlockwise	you are now facing
W	135°	anticlockwise	_____
SE	45°	clockwise	_____
NE	90°	anticlockwise	_____
SW	45°	anticlockwise	_____
S	180°	clockwise	_____

3 pencils and 4 ballpoint pens cost £1.70.
3 pencils and 2 ballpoint pens cost £1.30.
Use this information to find the cost of:

31 2 ballpoint pens _____   **32** 1 ballpoint pen _____

33 3 pencils _____   **34** 1 pencil _____

Divide each of the following numbers by 1000.

35 385 _____   **36** 0.12 _____

37 7.8 _____   **38** 49 _____

The population of Grangetown is 11 552. The men and children together number 8763, and the men and women number 5874.

39 How many women are there?   _____

40 There are _____ children.

41 How many men are there?   _____

Find the following:

42 The **factors** of 12 are 1, 2, _____, _____, _____ and _____ .

43 The **factors** of 20 are 1, _____, _____, _____, _____ and _____ .

44 The **factors** of 15 are _____, _____, _____ and _____ .

45 The numbers that are **factors** of both 12 and 20 are 1, _____ and _____ .

46 The numbers that are **factors** of both 12 and 15 are 1 and _____ .

47 The numbers that are **factors** of both 20 and 15 are 1 and _____ .

48–50 Now fill in the lengths of the sides of the box using these answers.

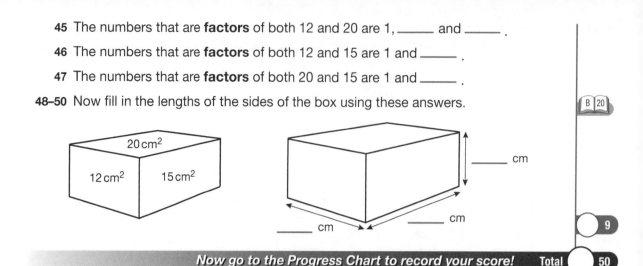

B 20

9

Now go to the Progress Chart to record your score!   Total   50

Paper 10

Look at these shapes.

B 24

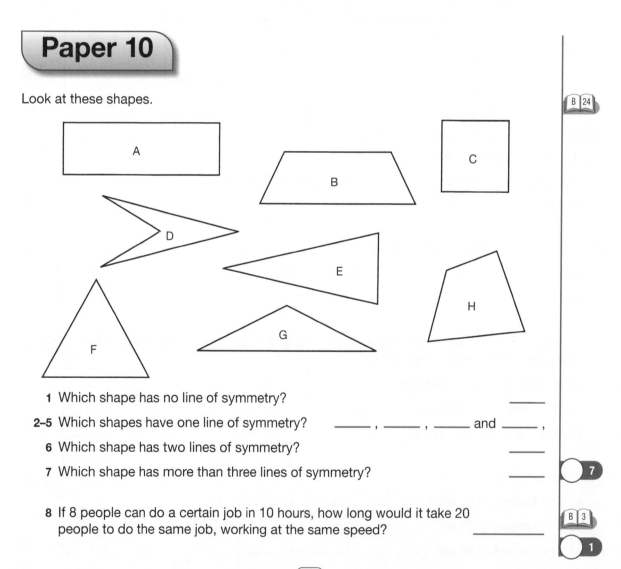

1 Which shape has no line of symmetry? _____

2–5 Which shapes have one line of symmetry?   _____ , _____ , _____ and _____ ,

6 Which shape has two lines of symmetry? _____

7 Which shape has more than three lines of symmetry? _____

7

8 If 8 people can do a certain job in 10 hours, how long would it take 20 people to do the same job, working at the same speed? _____

B 3

1

Find the **mean** of these sets of numbers.

9 7 11 4 6   _____

10 7 1 4 6 2   _____

11 7 11 4 6 2 12   _____   (3)

12 Thirty-six posts were spaced evenly along a road that was 1.575 km long.

What was the distance in metres between each pair of posts?   _____

B25/B3   (1)

13–19 Complete the following chart.

Wholesale price (Price at the factory)	Retail price (Price in the shop)	Profit (Money made by shopkeeper)
£7.85	£9.22	_____
_____	£17.10	£2.34
£38.75	_____	£5.67
£17.37	£21.14	_____
£41.85	_____	£8.19
_____	£67.76	£12.87
£0.87	_____	£0.18

(7)

B 23

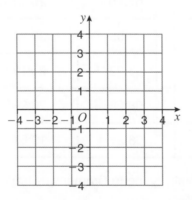

20–24 Plot the following **coordinates** on the chart and join them in the order you plot them.

(−3, −2) (−3, 3) (−1, 1) (1, 3) (1, −2)

25 What letter have you made?   _____   (6)

26–28 Emma (who is 8 years old), Salim (who is 7), and Katie (who is 5), share £10.00 in the ratio of their ages.

Emma gets _____ , Salim gets _____ and Katie gets _____ .

29 What must be added to 375 g to make 1 kg? _____ g

30 How many packets, each holding 125 g, can be filled from a case holding 3 kg? _____

Write these numbers as fractions in their **lowest terms**.

31 3.8   _____   **32** 11.4   _____

33 11.002 _____   **34** 3.25   _____

35 6.5   _____   **36** 1.12   _____

Mr and Mrs Black took their three children from Norwich to Cromer by train.

The tickets for the five people totalled £31.50.

All the children travelled at half price.

37 How much was an adult ticket? _____

	Train A	**Train B**	**Train C**	**Train D**
Norwich	06:15	07:33	20:48	22:10
Wroxham	06:26	07:48	20:32	21:54
Worstead	06:35	07:55	20:24	21:47
North Walsham	06:45	08:02	20:19	21:41
Gunton	06:51	08:08	20:09	21:35
Cromer	07:04	08:21	19:57	21:23

38 The fastest train for the Black family going to Cromer was train _____

39 The slowest train for the Black family returning to Norwich was train _____

40 If I leave Wroxham on the 07:48 train, and spend the day in Cromer, leaving on the 19:57 train, how long am I actually in Cromer?   ____ h ____ min

41 At what time does the 19:57 train from Cromer arrive in North Walsham?   _____

I live in Norwich and travel to Cromer on the 06:15 train, returning home on the 21:23 train.

42 How long will I spend travelling on the train that day? ____ h ____ min

43 At what time does the 20:09 from Gunton reach Wroxham? _____

6

44–46 In a sale all goods were reduced by 20%. Complete the chart below.

B12/B2

Ordinary price	Sale price
£20.00	_____
£35.00	_____
£60.00	_____

3

State whether the following statements are TRUE or FALSE.

B 17

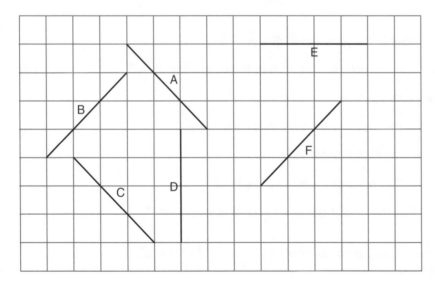

47 Line B is parallel to line A. _____

48 Line C is perpendicular to line F. _____

49 Line E is a horizontal line. _____

50 Line D is a vertical line. _____

4

Now go to the Progress Chart to record your score!   Total   50

27

Paper 11

This graph represents the journeys of a cyclist and a motorist. The motorist is faster than the cyclist.

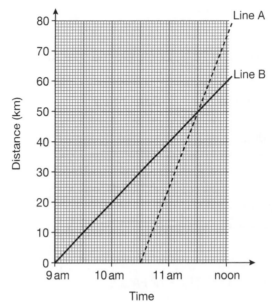

1 Which line represents the journey of the cyclist? _____

2 At what speed (km covered in 1 hour) was the cyclist travelling? _____ km/h

3 At what speed was the motorist travelling? _____ km/h

4 At what time did the motorist start his journey? _____

5 At what time did the cyclist start his journey? _____

6 At what time did the motorist overtake the cyclist? _____

7 How many km had the cyclist done when he was overtaken? _____

8 What would be the approximate cost of 13 films at £4.98 each (to the nearest £)? _____

9 The average of 4 numbers is $10\frac{1}{2}$.

If the average of 3 of them is 9, what is the 4th number? _____

10–14 Arrange these fractions in order of size, putting the largest first.

$\frac{1}{2}$ $\quad$ $\frac{2}{3}$ $\quad$ $\frac{5}{6}$ $\quad$ $\frac{3}{8}$ $\quad$ $\frac{3}{4}$

_____ _____ _____ _____ _____

Some children in a Youth Club made this Venn diagram to show which music they like.

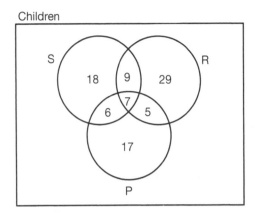

S = soul
R = rock
P = pop

15–17 _____ children like soul, _____ like rock and _____ like pop music.

18 The number of children who like both soul and rock is   _____

19 How many like both soul and pop?   _____

5

Here are three shaded cubes.

 A   B   C

Which cube has the following nets? Choose between A, B, C or none.

20
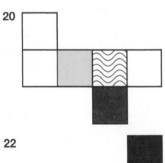   Is _____

21
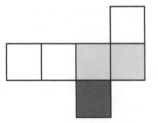   Is _____

22
   Is _____

23
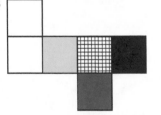   Is _____

24
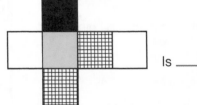   Is _____

5

Underline the correct answer in each line.

25 $\frac{1}{8} + \frac{1}{4}$ = $\frac{1}{12}$ $\frac{2}{12}$ $\frac{3}{8}$ $\frac{1}{4}$

26 2.00 − 1.77 = 0.33 0.23 3.77 1.23

27 0.3 × 0.3 = 0.09 0.6 0.06 0.33

28 3 ÷ 0.6 = 0.2 0.5 0.18 5

29–33 Plot the points (1, 3), (1, −1), (−3, −1) on the grid below.

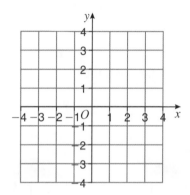

These points are the **vertices** of a square. Mark the fourth **vertex** and draw the square.

34–35 The **coordinates** of the fourth **vertex** are (_____, _____).

36–37 The **coordinates** of the centre of the square are (_____, _____).

Multiply each of the following by 100.

38 26.2 _____

39 8.9 _____

40 25.16 _____

41–43 A cash box contains some coins to the value of £5.25.

There are twice as many 5p coins as 2p coins, and twice as many 2p coins as 1p coins.

This means there are:

_____ 5p coins _____ 2p coins _____ 1p coins

1–5 The pie chart is divided into 8 equal sections to cover 120 minutes. Each section represents 15 minutes (120 minutes ÷ 8 segments = 15 minutes per segment).

1 **15** TV lasts for 1 segment x 15 minutes

2 **30** Homework lasts for 2 segments x 15 minutes

3 **30** Reading lasts for 2 segments x 15 minutes

4 **15** Washing up lasts for 1 segment x 15 minutes

5 **30** Computer time lasts for 2 segment x 15 minutes

6–8 To find the mean of a set of numbers, add the numbers together and then divide the total by the quantity of numbers in the group.

6 **6** 7 + 4 + 6 + 8 + 5 = 30; 30 ÷ 5 = 6

7 **4** 3 + 2 + 7 = 12; 12 ÷ 3 = 4

8 **4** 4 + 4 + 6 + 2 = 16; 16 ÷ 4 = 4

9 **9990** To multiply by 10, place the numbers on a decimal grid with a 9 in the hundreds, a 9 in the tens and a 9 in the ones (units) column. To make a number larger, move the numbers to the left. There is now a 9 in the thousands, a 9 in the hundreds and a 9 in the tens columns. There is nothing in the ones column, so place a zero in it.

thousands	hundreds	tens	units
9	9	9	0

10–19 To solve this type of question, make all the fractions and decimals equivalent (for example, $\frac{5}{8}$, $\frac{3}{4}$ = $\frac{6}{8}$, $\frac{7}{8}$, $\frac{6}{8}$, $\frac{1}{2}$ = $\frac{4}{8}$ or 0.125, $\frac{1}{2}$ = 0.5, 0.25, $\frac{7}{8}$ = 0.875, 0.75) and then order them.

10–11 $\frac{1}{2}$ (smallest); $\frac{7}{8}$

12–13 **0.307** (smallest); **37** (largest)

14–15 $\frac{10}{10}$ (smallest); $\frac{15}{3}$ (largest)

16–17 **0.125** (smallest); $\frac{7}{8}$ (largest)

18–19 $\frac{2}{5}$ of 10 (smallest); $\frac{5}{7}$ of 14 (largest)

20 **102021**

21–24 The function machine multiplies each number by 10 and then subtracts 1.

21 **169** 17 x 10 = 170; 170 − 1 = 169

22 **209** 21 x 10 = 210; 210 − 1 = 209

23 **389** 39 x 10 = 390; 390 − 1 = 389

24 **449** 45 x 10 = 450; 450 − 1 = 449

25–27 Each quarter is 90° and contains 3 numbers, so each number is equal to 30° (90° ÷ 3 = 30°).

25 **60°** 2 x 30° = 60°

26 **150°** 5 x 30° = 150°

27 **120°** 4 hours x 30° = 120°

28 **NOT gloss washable paint** If the answer to the question 'It is gloss?' is 'Yes' and that makes 'Gloss washable paint', then if the answer is 'No' it must make 'NOT gloss washable paint'. It is clear from the earlier

question that the paint is washable, regardless of whether it is gloss or not.

29 **Is it gloss?** The 'Yes' answer to the missing question points to 'Gloss washable paint'. This answer only differs in one way from the 'No' answer: it is described as 'Gloss' while the 'No' answer is described as 'NOT gloss'. The missing question must therefore be asking whether the paint is gloss or not.

30–33 This is BIDMAS. Complete the equation in the brackets first, then the multiplication or division, then the addition or subtraction.

30 **5** (7 x 8) + 5 = 61; 7 x 8 = 56 then 61 − 56 = 5

31 **2** (9 x 12) − 2 = 106; 9 x 12 = 108 then 108 − 106 = 2

32 **3** 8 x (7 − 3) = 32; 8 x 4 = 32 then 7 − 4 = 3

33 **5** 6 x (11 − 5) = 36; 6 x 6 = 36 then 11 − 6 = 5

34–38 When plotting coordinates on a grid, use the rule "along the corridor and up the stairs" to remember to go horizontal, then vertical.

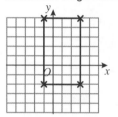

38 **(−1, −2)**

39–41 There are 60 minutes in an hour, so a quarter of an hour is 15 minutes. Subtract this from the times given to get the correct answer.

39 **21:45**   40 **10:50**   41 **12:55**

42–44 To solve a ratio, add up the ratio numbers (1 + 3 + 5 = 9). Then divide this number into the number of pencils (36 ÷ 9 = 4). Finally, multiply this number by the individual ratios.

42 **4** 4 x 1   43 **12** 4 x 3   44 **20** 4 x 5

45–48 When filling in a missing symbol, you can check your answer by reversing the equation. The reversals are shown in brackets below.

45 **+** (52 − 7 = 45)   46 **÷** (33 ÷ 11 = 3)

47 **x** (37 968 ÷ 678 = 56)   48 **÷** (18 x 5 = 90)

49 **24 cm²** Picture the shape as 2 rectangles. The top rectangle is 6 cm wide and 2 cm high. Multiply these two numbers to get the area (6 cm x 2 cm = 12 cm²). Now find the area of the bottom rectangle. The total height of the shape is 8 cm and the top rectangle is 2 cm, so the bottom rectangle must be 6 cm high (8 cm − 2 cm = 6 cm). The rectangle is 2 across, so multiplying the length and width gives 12 cm². Add the areas of the 2 rectangles to get the total area (12 cm² + 12 cm² = 24 cm²).

50 **28 cm** To find the perimeter, first add the missing measurements to the diagram. Working out Question 49 showed that the

sides of the bottom part of the 'T' are 6 cm each. The two sections on the underside of the crossbar must add up to 4 cm (6 cm – 2 cm = 4 cm). The next step is to add up all the measurements (6 cm + 2 cm + 2 cm + 6 cm + 2 cm + 6 cm + 2 cm + 2 cm = 28 cm).

Paper 2 (pages 4–6)

1–4 To divide by 10, place the numbers in a decimal grid using hundreds, tens, units, tenths, hundredths, thousandths, etc. Reduce a number by 10 by moving it 1 place to the right.

1 **7.865**

T	U	.	t	h	th
7	8	.	6	5	
	7	.	8	6	5

2 **0.654**

T	U	.	t	h	th
	6	.	5	4	
	0	.	6	5	4

3 **46.75**

H	T	U	.	t	h
4	6	7	.	5	
	4	6	.	7	5

4 **0.0123**

U	.	t	h	th	tth
0	.	1	2	3	
0	.	0	1	2	3

5–8 **49, 47, 45, 43** A quotient is the answer when you divide one number by another. First work out all the division problems (315 ÷ 7 = 45; 392 ÷ 8 = 49; 329 ÷ 7 = 47; 387 ÷ 9 = 43) and then put the quotients in order from highest to lowest.

9–10 **185 boys; 222 girls** For every 11 children, if 6 are girls, then 5 are boys (11 – 6 = 5). Divide the total number of children in the school by 11 (407 ÷ 11 = 37). That means there are 37 groups of 11 children in the school, each with 5 boys and 6 girls. Multiply each number by 37 (5 x 37; 6 x 37) to find the total numbers of boys and girls.

11–14 To use the conversion graph, remember that the miles are read on the vertical line (y axis) and the kilometres are read on the bottom horizontal line (x axis).

11–12 **Darlington 40 km; Newcastle 80 km** Look at the vertical axis and find 25 miles (midway between 20 and 30). Follow the line across to the right until reaching the diagonal line. Then read down to find that 25 miles is the same as 40 kilometres. To convert the other figure,

follow the same process. Another way of working it out would would be to use doubling: if 25 miles = 40 km then doubling both shows that 50 miles = 80 kilometres.

13 **60 miles** Find 95 km on the horizontal line. Follow it upwards until it touches the diagonal line, then read across to find 60 miles.

14 **50 miles** Find 75 km on the horizontal line. Follow it upwards until it touches the diagonal line, then read across. 75 km = 45 miles, so 50 miles is greater.

15–18 When filling in a missing symbol, you can check your answer by reversing the equation. The reversals are shown in brackets below.

15 ÷ (5 x 14.8 = 74)   16 + (79 – 5 = 74)
17 – (69 + 5 = 74)   18 x (370 ÷ 5 = 74)

19–21 To find the probability it is helpful to write out the 6 balls (1, 2, 3, 4, 5, 6) and then use those numbers to answer the questions.

19 $\frac{1}{2}$ There are 3 even-numbered balls out of a total of 6, and $\frac{3}{6} = \frac{1}{2}$.

20 $\frac{1}{6}$ There is 1 ball numbered '5' out of a total of 6.

21 $\frac{1}{2}$ There are 3 odd-numbered balls out of a total of 6, and $\frac{3}{6} = \frac{1}{2}$.

22–24 A prime number can only be divided by itself and 1. The prime numbers here are **3, 5** and **7.**

25–26 To find a midway number, add the two numbers together and then divide by 2.

25 **30** 18 + 42 = 60; 60 ÷ 2 = 30

26 **36** 19 + 53 = 72; 72 ÷ 2 = 36

27 **9 cm²** First, find the length of each side. All four sides of a square are identical in length, so 12 cm ÷ 4 = 3 cm. Area is found by multiplying length x width, so 3 x 3 = 9 cm².

28–31 To use a world time chart, begin with the first country and add or subtract the number of hours to find the time in another country.

28 **03:00** Japan is +9 hours from London, so to find the time in London when it is midday in Japan, subtract 9 hours (12:00 – 9 hours = 03:00).

29 **11:00** Japan is +1 hour from Hong Kong (Hong Kong is +8 from London and Japan is +9, so there is a 1-hour difference). To find the time in Hong Kong when it is midday in Japan, subtract 1 hour (12:00 – 1 hour = 11:00).

30 **11:00** Cyprus is +2 hours from London and Austria is +1 hour, so there is a 1-hour difference. If it is midday in Cyprus, subtract 1 hour to find the time in Austria (12:00 – 1 hour = 11:00).

31 **8:36 a.m.** Hong Kong is +8 hours from London, so if it is 4:36 p.m. in Hong Kong, then subtract 8 hours to find the time in London (4:36 p.m. – 8 hours = 8:36 a.m.).

32 $\frac{1}{2}$ The coin has 2 sides (1 head and 1 tail), with an equal chance of landing on each.

33 $\frac{1}{2}$ As there are 2 sides, the chance of getting a tail is the same as the chance of getting a head.

34–35 There are 5 increments between 6.3 and 6.4. Take the difference between these numbers (6.4 − 6.3 = 1.0) and divide it by the number of increments (1 ÷ 5 = 0.2). Then label each increment (e.g. 6.34, 6.34, 6.36, 6.38).

34 6.34   **35 6.42**

36–37 To add fractions together, first find equivalent fractions so that the bottom numbers (the denominators) are the same. Remember to only add the top numbers (the numerators), not the denominators. Then put the answer in its simplest form by dividing the numerator and denominator by the same number, making both numbers as small as possible.

36 $1\frac{1}{16}$ $\frac{5}{8} = \frac{10}{16}; \frac{10}{16} + \frac{7}{16} = \frac{17}{16}; \frac{17}{16} = 1\frac{1}{16}$

37 $2\frac{7}{9}$ $7 = \frac{63}{9}; 4\frac{2}{9} = \frac{38}{9}; \frac{63}{9} - \frac{38}{9} = \frac{25}{9}; \frac{25}{9} = 2\frac{7}{9}$

38 20 cards For every 5 cards that Thomas has, Matthew will have 4 cards. If Matthew has 16 cards then divide this by 4 (16 ÷ 4 = 4). This shows that Matthew has his share of 4 cards multiplied by 4. Thomas' share will also be multiplied by 4 (5 x 4 = 20).

39 18 cards If Matthew has 16 cards and Thomas has 20 cards, there are 36 cards in total. Shared out equally, they would each receive 18 (36 ÷ 2 = 18).

40–43 To find the median of a set of numbers, list the numbers in order, from smallest to largest, then take the middle number.

40 3 (1, 3, 8)   **41 20** (11, 20, 34)   **42 3** (3, 3, 4)

43 6 There is an even number of numbers, so there are two numbers in the middle (5 and 7). Find the number midway between these two (6).

44–46 To write these fractions as decimals, separate them from the whole number first, then write the equivalent of each fraction so that the bottom number becomes 100. Write the top number of the equivalent fraction after the decimal point. Add this back to the whole number.

44 4.50 $\frac{1}{2} = \frac{50}{100}; \frac{50}{100} = 0.50; 4 + 0.50 = 4.50$

45 7.1 $\frac{1}{10} = \frac{10}{100}; \frac{10}{100} = 0.10; 0.10 + 7 = 7.10$

46 3.09 $\frac{9}{100} = 0.09; 0.09 + 3 = 3.09$

47–50 There are different strategies for solving any of these questions, but here is the working out method recommended by the National Curriculum.

	8	8	7
	9	9	8
+	7	7	6
2	**6**	**6**	**1**
2	2	2	

	3	7	8
x			9
3	4	0	2
	7	7	

	0	2	3	4
	2	²8	⁴0	⁴8
	2	4		
		4	0	
		3	6	
			4	8
			4	8
				0

			4	5	6
				3	5
1	3	6	8	0	
	1	1			
	2	2	8	0	
	2	3			
1	5	9	6	0	
	1				

Paper 3 (pages 7–9)

1 4 $4^2 = 2 \times 2 = 4$ **2 25** $5^2 = 5 \times 5 = 25$

3 9 $3^2 = 3 \times 3 = 9$ **4 36** $6^2 = 6 \times 6 = 36$

5–15 Start with the time given and add or subtract to work out the other times. For example, if break ends at 1:10 and the break lasts for 15 minutes, then it begins at 12:55 The time a lesson ends is the same time as the start of the next lesson.

	Begins	Ends
1st lesson	11:10	11:45
2nd lesson	11:45	12:20
3rd lesson	12:20	12:55
Break	12:55	1:10
4th lesson	1:10	1:45
5th lesson	1:45	2:20

16 988 Divide 1000 by 38 and round down the answer to the nearest whole number. Then multiply this number by 38.

17–22 To find the area, multiply the base by the height. To find the perimeter, add the length of each of the sides together.

17 60 cm² 10 cm × 6 cm = 60 cm²

18 30 cm² 5 cm × 6 cm = 30 cm²

19 50 cm² 5 cm × 10 cm = 50 cm²

20 32 cm 10 cm + 6 cm + 10 cm + 6 cm = 32 cm

21 22 cm 5 cm + 6 cm + 5 cm + 6 cm = 22 cm

22 30 cm 10 cm + 5 cm + 10 cm + 5 cm = 30 cm

23–26 To solve this type of question, work out the calculation on the right-hand side of the equation. This will be equal to the calculation on the left-hand side of the equation.

23 **10** 2 × 10 = 4 × 5; 4 × 5 = 20 and 2 × 10 = 20

24 **5** 5 × 25 = 27 − 2; 27 − 2 = 25 and 5 × 5 = 25

25 **4** 12 × 3 = 36 ÷ 3; 36 ÷ 3 = 12 and 4 × 3 = 12

26 **5** 5 × 4 = 10 + 10; 10 + 10 = 20 and 5 × 4 = 20

27–28 To solve a ratio, add up the ratio numbers (11 + 9 = 20). Then divide this number into the total sum of money (£40 ÷ 20 = £2). Finally, multiply this number by the individual ratios.

27 **£22** £2 × 11   28 **£18** £2 × 9

29 **£5.36** Divide the total cost by 11 to find the cost of a single item (£7.37 ÷ 11 = £0.67). Then multiply this number by 8 (£0.67 × 8 = £5.36).

30–33 To find the area of a triangle, multiply the height by the length and then divide by 2.

30 **6 cm²** 4 squares long × 3 squares high = 12 cm²; 12 cm² ÷ 2 = 6 cm²

31 **12 cm²** 6 squares long × 4 squares high = 24 cm²; 24 cm² ÷ 2 = 12 cm²

32 **10 cm²** 4 squares long × 5 squares high = 20 cm²; 20 cm² ÷ 2 = 10 cm²

33 **12 cm²** 6 squares long × 4 squares high = 24 cm²; 24 cm² ÷ 2 = 12 cm²

34–37 Work out the total time parked by subtracting the arrival time from the departure time. Then use the chart to work out the payment required.

34 **£3.50** 4 p.m. – 12:30 p.m. = 3 hours 30 minutes, which is over 2 hours and up to 4 hours.

35 **£3.50** 11:30 a.m. – 9:15 a.m. = 2 hours 15 minutes, which is over 2 hours and up to 4 hours.

36 **£5.25** 6:30 p.m. – 2:20 p.m. = 4 hours 10 minutes, which is over 4 hours and up to 6 hours.

37 **£7.00** 4:30 p.m. – 8:45 a.m. = 7 hours 45 minutes, which is over 6 hours and under 8 hours.

38–43 First, work out 20% of the prices provided. An easy way to do this is to work out 10% (by dividing by 10) and then doubling the result. This gives the VAT, which can be added to the 'Price Before VAT' to give the 'Total cost'.

38–39 10% of £180 is £18; £18 × 2 = £36; £180 + £36 = £216.00

40–41 10% of £420 is £42; £42 × 2 = £84; £420 + £84 = £504.00

42–43 10% of £340 is £34; £34 × 2 = £68; £340 + £68 = £408.00

Price before VAT	VAT	Total cost
£180.00	£36.00	£216.00
£420.00	£84.00	£504.00
£340.00	£68.00	£408.00

44–46 There are different strategies for solving any of these questions but here is the working out method recommended by the National Curriculum:

	m		c	m
	4		7	2
+	3		3	9
	8		1	1
	1		1	

	m		cm
		5	
	6		¹2
−	3		8
	2		4

	m		c	m
	4		6	0
x				5
2	3		0	0
	3			

47–50 When rounding a number to the nearest 100, look at the number in the tens column. If it is 4 or below, leave the number in the hundreds column unchanged. If it is 5 or above, raise the number in the hundreds column by 1.

47 **300** The 90 in 298 rounds up to 300.

48 **800** The 40 in 847 rounds down to 800.

49 **500** The 00 in 503 round down to 500.

50 **1100** The 70 in 1074 rounds up to 1100.

Paper 4 (pages 9–11)

1–5 The perimeter of a rectangle can be found by adding up the 2 lengths and the 2 widths. For a square, the length and width are the same.

	Length	Width	Perimeter
Rectangle 1	18 cm	**2 cm**	40 cm
Rectangle 2	**12 cm**	3 cm	30 cm
Rectangle 3	9 cm	4 cm	**26 cm**
Square	6 cm	**6 cm**	**24 cm**

6 **47** 1316 ÷ 28 = 47

7 **0.01** Multiplying a number by 0.1 makes it 10 times smaller.

8 **4** To find 10%, divide by 10 (40 ÷ 10 = 4).

9 **0.01** A quick way of subtracting 9.99 from 10 is to imagine the sum is money (£10 − £9.99 = £0.01).

10 **0.69** To divide by a decimal fraction, it is easier to make that number a whole number. Multiply both the decimal fraction and the number you are dividing into by the same power of 10. 0.207 ÷ 0.3 is the same as 2.07 ÷ 3 = 0.69.

11 **1.21** First work out 11 × 11 = 121. Now count how many digits are after the decimal points in the question (in 1.1 × 1.1 there are 2) and make sure the same number of digits are after the decimal point in the answer. So 1.1 × 1.1 = 1.21

12 **5.67** To divide by 100, place the numbers in a decimal grid using tens, units, tenths, hundredths etc. Reduce a number by 100 by moving it 2 places to the right.

13 **36** A product is found by multiplying numbers together. One of the numbers is 35, so divide 1260 by 35 to find the other number (1260 ÷ 35 = 36).

14–20 Use logic to work out the missing digits, then solve the equation to check if the answer works.

14–16 Find the 7 by working out what must be added to 6 (5 + 1 = 6) to make a number ending in 3. Remembering to carry the 1 from 13, 1 + 6 + 5 = 12, so 8 must be added to 12 to make a number ending in 6. Carrying the 2, 2 + 3 + 4 = 9, so 7 must be added to make a number ending in 6. Carrying the 1, 1 + 2+ 3 = 6, so 4 must be added to get 10.

	4	3	6	5
	2	7	8	1
+	3	4	5	7
1	0	6	0	3
	1	2	1	

17–18 Find the 1 by working out what number, subtract 5, gives 6. Remembering that 1 has been borrowed from the 7 to make 11, 16 – 8 = 8, so 8 must be subtracted to give 8. 10 – 1 (borrowed to make 16) – 2 = 7, so the last missing number must be 0.

	0	9	16	1
	~~1~~	~~0~~	~~7~~	1
–		2	8	5
		7	8	6

19 Start by estimating the answer. 2000 × 300 = 7, so try 7.

		3	4	5
	×			7
	2	4	1	5
		3	3	

20 9 × 38 = 342. Check the answer by working out the division.

	0	3	8
9	3	³4	⁷2

21 **3** Complete the subtraction first (10 – 1 = 9). That gives 3y = 9, so 9 ÷ 3 = y. 9 ÷ 3 = 3, so y = 3.

22 **4** Complete the subtraction first (4y – y = 3y). That gives 3y = 12, so 12 ÷ 3 = y. 12 ÷ 3 = 4, so y = 4.

23 **2** Complete the subtraction first (2y + y = 3y). That gives 3y = 6, so 6 ÷ 3 = y. 6 ÷ 3 = 2, so y = 2.

24 **3** Complete the subtractions first (3y + y = 4y and 11 + 1 = 12). That gives 4y = 12, so 12 ÷ 4 = y. 12 ÷ 4 = 3, so y = 3.

25–26 There are 5 increments between 9.9 and 10.0. Take the difference between these numbers (10.0 – 9.9 = 0.1) and divide it by the number of increments (0.1 ÷ 5 = 0.02). Then label each increments (e.g. 9.92, 9.94, 9.96, 9.98).

25 **9.98**   **26** **10.06**

27–29 To find out the probability it is helpful to write out the 6 possible scores (1, 2, 3, 4, 5, 6) and then use those numbers to answer the questions.

27 $\frac{1}{6}$ There is 1 side numbered 6 out of a total of 6.

28 $\frac{1}{6}$ There is 1 side numbered 5 out of a total of 6.

29 $\frac{2}{6}$ or $\frac{1}{3}$ There are 2 sides numbered 2 or 3 out of a total of 6.

30–32 To solve a number square, take any complete row and work out the sequence between the numbers. Then use the same sequence to find the missing numbers.

30 **46** In the first row (38, 34, 30) the sequence is to take away 4. If this sequence is applied to the last row (x, 42, 38), x must be 4 greater than 42, so the answer is 46.

31 **138** In the middle row (84, 102, 120) the sequence is to add 18. If this sequence is applied to the first row (102, 120, y), y must be 18 greater than 120, so the answer is 138.

32 **23** In the middle row (27, 31, 35) the sequence is to add 4. If this sequence is applied to the first row (z, 27, 31), z must be 4 less than 27, so the answer is 23.

33–38 To multiply by 10, place the numbers on a decimal grid using thousands, hundreds, tens, units, tenths, hundreds, thousandths, etc. Increase a number by 10 by moving it one place to the left. If necessary, place a zero in the units columns.

33 **37.7**   **34** **465**   **35** **1.26**   **36** **0.27**
37 **490**   **38** **5670**   **39** **0.023**

40–45 To find the median of a set of numbers, put the numbers in order from smallest to largest. The median is the middle number. If there are 2 middle numbers, add the 2 numbers together and then divide by 2.

40 **7** 4, 6, 8, 10; 6 + 8 = 14; 14 ÷ 2 = 7

41 **7** 2, 6, 8, 8; 6 + 8 = 14; 14 ÷ 2 = 7

42 **20** 7, 19, 21, 54; 19 + 21 = 40; 40 ÷ 2 = 20

43 **3.5 or $3\frac{1}{2}$** 1, 2, 3, 4, 5, 6; 3 + 4 = 7; 7 ÷ 2 = 3.5 or $3\frac{1}{2}$

44 **19** 3, 5, 17, 21, 32, 60; 17 + 21 = 38; 38 ÷ 2 = 19

45 **46** 45, 47; 45 + 47 = 92; 92 ÷ 2 = 46

46–50 In 24-hour time, 0:00–11:59 represent the times from midnight to midday (a.m.) and 12:01–23:59 represent the times from midday to midnight (p.m.). To change from 24-hour to 12-hour time, if the time begins with a number between 1 and 11, write 'a.m' after the time. If the time begins with a number between 13 and 23, subtract 12 from it to get the new time. If the time begins with 00, then it is 12am; if it begins with 12, then it is 12pm.

Paper 5 (pages 11–14)

1–7 The area of a rectangle can be found by multiplying the length by the width. To find the length or width, divide the area by the given dimension.

	Length	Width	Area
Rectangle 1	8 m	6 m	**48 m²**
Rectangle 2	**8 m**	4 m	32 m²
Rectangle 3	4 m	**2,5 m**	10 m²
Rectangle 4	**3 m**	3.5 m	10.5 m²
Rectangle 5	1.5 m	1.5 m	**2.25 m²**
Rectangle 6	5 m	**1.2 m**	6 m²
Rectangle 7	1.3 m	2 m	**2.6 m²**

8–11 To find the area of a triangle, multiply the height by the length and then divide by 2. Use the perpendicular height, measuring a straight line from the top point of the triangle to its base. Remember that a triangle can be rotated in any direction.

8 15 cm² 5 squares long × 6 squares high = 30 cm²; 30 cm² ÷ 2 = 15 cm²

9 30 cm² 10 squares long × 6 squares high = 60 cm²; 60 cm² ÷ 2 = 30 cm²

10 16 cm² 8 squares long × 4 squares high = 32 cm²; 32 cm² ÷ 2 = 16 cm²

11 10 cm² 5 squares long × 4 squares high = 20 cm²; 20 cm² ÷ 2 = 10 cm²

12 7:58 p.m. The watch loses 1 whole minute every 4 hours. Between midday and 8 p.m. there are 8 hours. 8 – 4 = 2 minutes. The watch is losing time, so subtract 2 minutes from 8 p.m. 8 p.m. – 2 minutes = 7:58 p.m.

13 Mathematics With 12, Mathematics has more votes than any of the others.

14 English With 5 votes, English has fewer votes than any of the others.

15 30 5 + 12 + 7 + 6 = 30

16 7.5 To find the mean of a set of a numbers, divide the total of votes (30) by the number of subjects (English, Mathematics, PE, Music); 30 ÷ 4 = 7.5.

17 4 When the symbol represents 2 then 2 × 2 = 4

18 8 When the symbol represents 4 then 2 × 4 = 8

19 12 When the symbol represents 6 then 2 × 6 = 12

20 16 When the symbol represents 8 then 2 × 8 = 16

21 20 When the symbol represents 10 then 2 × 10 = 20

22 24 When the symbol represents 12 then 2 × 12 = 24

23–28 To reduce a price by 10%, divide the price by 10, then subtract this from the original price.

23 £45 £50 ÷ 10 = £5; £50 – £5 = £45

24 £99 £110 ÷ 10 = £11; £110 – £11 = £99

25 £225 £250 ÷ 10 = £25; £250 – £25 = £225

26 £36 £40 ÷ 10 = £4; £40 – £4 = £36

27 £27 £30 ÷ 10 = £3; £30 – £3 = £27

28 £252 £280 ÷ 10 = £28; £280 – £28 = £252

29–30 288, 72 To find 20%, work out 10% (by dividing by 10) and double the result (360 ÷ 10 = 36; 36 × 2 = 72). This is the number of children who were on the museum trip. Subtract the number of children who were on the museum trip from the total number of children to find the number of children who in school (360 – 72 = 288).

31 4 4 × 4 = 16

32 $14.60 If $1.46 is equal to £1, multiply both numbers by 10 to find out how many dollars there are for £10 ($1.46 × 10 = 14.6).

33 11 900 If 119 shillings is equal to £1, multiply both numbers by 100 to find out how many shillings there are for £100 (119 × 100 = 11 900).

34 €1160 If €1.16 is equal to £1, multiply both numbers by 1000 to find out how many euros there are for £1000 (1.16 × 1000 = 1160).

35 $\frac{3}{7}$ There are 3 white balls out of a total of 4 + 3 = 7 balls.

36 $\frac{4}{7}$ There are 4 grey balls out of a total of 7 balls.

37 0 There are 0 black balls out of a total of 7 balls.

38 137 11 × 12 + 5 = 137

39 9:13 p.m. Add 1 hour 35 minutes to 7:30 p.m. (7:30 p.m. + 1 hour = 8:30 p.m.; 8:30 p.m. + 35 minutes = 9:05 p.m.). Then add 8 minutes (9:05 p.m. + 8 minutes = 9:13 p.m.).

40–42 Use a to represent the width of the rectangular field. The length is 3 times the width, or $3a$. So the perimeter is $a + 3a + a + 3a = 8a$. The perimeter is 0.8 km, so $8a = 0.8$km. This means a is 0.1 km.

40 0.3 km The length is $3a$ and a is 0.1 km, so the length is 0.1 km × 3 = 0.3 km.

41 0.1 km The width is a so the width is 0.1 km.

42 0.03 km To find the area of a rectangle, multiply the length by the width (0.1 km × 0.3 km = 0.03 km).

43 12 days If there is enough food to last 2 dogs for 18 days, there is enough food to last 1 dog for 2 × 18 = 36 days. So there is enough food to last 3 dogs for 36 ÷ 3 = 12 days.

44 1221 665 + 556 = 1221

45 74 To find the number halfway between two numbers, add the 2 numbers together and then divide by 2 (37 + 111 = 148; 148 ÷ 2 = 74).

46 13   **47 17**

48–50 To find the prime factors of a number, divide by prime numbers. Try each prime number in turn, starting with the smallest, until the result is also prime. $60 \div 2 = 30$; $30 \div 2 = 15$; $15 \div 3 = 5$. The prime factors of 60 are 2 and 3 and 5.

Paper 6 (pages 14–16)

1–3 The function machine multiplies each number by 2 and then adds 3.
1 **37** $17 \times 2 = 34$; $34 + 3 = 37$
2 **121** $59 \times 2 = 118$; $118 + 3 = 121$
3 **95** $46 \times 2 = 92$; $92 + 3 = 95$
4–8 To find the size of the internal angle of a shape, divide 360° by the number of angles at the centre.
4 **120°** $360° \div 3 = 120°$ **5** **90°** $360° \div 4 = 90°$
6 **72°** $360° \div 5 = 72°$ **7** **60°** $360° \div 6 = 60°$
8 **45°** $360° \div 8 = 45°$
9–11 There are 100 centimetres in a metre, so to convert centimetres to metres, divide by 100.
9 **2.45** $245 \text{ cm} \div 100 = 2.45 \text{ m}$
10 **13.42** $1342 \text{ cm} \div 100 = 13.42 \text{ m}$
11 **123.45** $12\,345 \text{ cm} \div 100 = 123.45 \text{ m}$
12–14 There are 1000 metres in a kilometre, so to convert metres to kilometres, divide by 1000.
12 **1.357** $1357 \text{ m} \div 1000 = 1.357 \text{ km}$
13 **12.986** $12\,986 \text{ m} \div 1000 = 12.986 \text{ km}$
14 **0.456** $456 \text{ m} \div 1000 = 0.456 \text{ km}$
15–16 **18, 12** To find 60%, work out 10% (by dividing by 60) and multiply the result by 6 ($30 \div 10 = 3$; $3 \times 6 = 18$). This is the number of girls. Subtract the number of girls from the total number of children to find the number of boys ($30 - 18 = 12$).
17 **17** $51 \times 10 = 510$; $510 \div 30 = 17$
18 **1993** $2000 - 7 = 1993$
19–34

35 **£7.70** Divide the total cost by 9 to find the cost of a single item (£6.30 ÷ 9 = £0.70). Then multiply this number by 11 (£0.70 × 11 = £7.70).
36–41 When rounding a number to the nearest 1000, look at the number in the hundreds column. If it is 4 or below, leave the number in the thousands columns unchanged. If it is 5 or above, raise the number in the thousands columns by 1.
36 **7000** The 500 in 6516 rounds up to 7000.
37 **6000** The 300 in 6380 rounds down to 6000.

38 **7000** The 600 in 6695 rounds up to 7000.
39 **5000** The 500 in 4500 rounds up to 5000.
40 **6000** The 000 in 6019 rounds down to 6000.
41 **5000** The 600 in 4667 rounds up to 5000.
42–47 < is less than, > is greater than
42 **=** $8 \times 9 = 72$ and $6 \times 12 = 72$; $72 = 72$
43 **<** $8 + 9 + 7 = 24$ and $30 - 3 = 27$; $24 < 27$
44 **>** 0.5 m = 50 cm; 50 cm > 45 cm
45 **>** $3^2 = 9$; $23 > 9$ **46** **=** $12^2 = 144$; $144 = 144$
47 **>** $\frac{3}{4}$ hour = 45 minutes; 50 min > 45 min
48–50 To find probability it is helpful to write out the 6 possible scores (1, 2, 3, 4, 5, 6) and then use those numbers to answer the questions.
48 $\frac{1}{3}$ There are two sides numbered 4 or 5 out of a total of 6, and $\frac{2}{6} = \frac{1}{3}$.
49 **0** There are no sides numbered 7, so this is impossible.
50 **1** There are 6 sides numbered 1, 2, 3, 4, 5 and 6, so this is certain.

Paper 7 (pages 16–19)

1 **0.04** $2 \times 2 = 4$. There are 2 numbers after the decimal points in the question, so there must be 2 numbers after the decimal point in the answer ($0.2 \times 0.2 = 0.04$).
2 $\frac{3}{4}$ $\left(\frac{1}{2} = \frac{2}{4}, \frac{2}{4} + \frac{1}{4} = \frac{3}{4}\right)$.
3 **15** 50% is half, so divide by 2 ($30 \div 2 = 15$).
4 **20** Dividing by $\frac{1}{2}$ is the same as multiplying by 2 ($10 \times 2 = 20$).
5 **10** $0.5 = \frac{1}{2}$ and dividing by $\frac{1}{2}$ is the same as multiplying by 2 ($5 \times 2 = 10$).
6 **103** $412 \div 4 = 103$
7 $\frac{5}{8}$ $\left(\frac{1}{2} = \frac{4}{8}, \frac{1}{8} + \frac{4}{8} = \frac{5}{8}\right)$.
8 **8:00**
Bus A: 7:00, 7:05, 7:10, 7:15, 7:20, 7:25, 7:30, 7:35, 7:40, 7:45, 7:50, 7:55, 8:00
Bus B: 7:00, 7:15, 7:30, 7:45, 8:00
Bus C: 7:00, 7:12, 7:24, 7:36, 7:48, 8:00
9 **23 000** The 800 in 22 837 rounds up to 23 000.
10 **29 000** The 000 in 29 029 rounds down to 29 000.
11 **28 000** The 200 in 28 251 rounds down to 28 000.
12 **19 000** The 300 in 19 336 rounds down to 19 000.
13 **20 000** The 300 in 20 320 rounds down to 20 000.
14 **16 000** The 700 in 15 782 rounds up to 16 000.
15 **18** $15 \times 12 = 180$; $180 \div 10 = 18$
16–18 **80, 40, 20** For every 1 app that Andrew has, Stuart has 2 and Meena has 4. This gives the ratio 1 : 2 : 4. To solve a ratio, add up the ratio numbers ($1 + 2 + 4 = 7$). Then divide this number into the number of apps ($140 \div 7 = 20$). Finally, multiply this number by the individual ratios (Andrew has $1 \times 20 = 20$; Stuart has $2 \times 20 = 40$; Meena has $4 \times 20 = 80$).

19 **35** To find the mean of a set of numbers, add the numbers together and then divide the total by the quantity of numbers in the group (36 + 33 + 37 + 34 + 35 = 175; 175 ÷ 5 = 35).

20 **36** To find the median, list the numbers in order from smallest to largest (36, 36, 36, 38, 39). The median is the middle number.

21 **36** The mode is the most popular value. 36 children attended on 3 afternoons, so the mode is 36.

22–26 To multiply by 1000, place the numbers in a decimal grid using tens, units, tenths, hundredths, thousandths, etc.) To make a number 1000 larger, move the numbers 3 places to the left.

22 **37,800** 37.8 × 1000 = 37,800

23 **2450** 2.45 × 1000 = 2450

24 **47** 0.047 × 1000 = 47

25 **25 000** 25.0 × 1000 = 25 000

26 **820** 0.82 × 1000 = 820

27 **$13\frac{11}{16}$** To add fractions together, first find equivalent fractions so that the bottom numbers (the denominators) are the same. Remember to only add the top numbers (the numerators), not the denominators. Deal with the whole numbers separately. $\left(7\frac{7}{8} + 5\frac{13}{16} = 7 + 5 + \frac{7}{8} + \frac{13}{16} = 12 + \frac{14}{16} + \frac{13}{16} = 12 + \frac{27}{16} = 12 + 1 + \frac{11}{16} = 13\frac{11}{16}\right)$.

28 **$3\frac{7}{15}$** $\left(7\frac{1}{5} - 3\frac{11}{15} = \frac{36}{5} - \frac{56}{15} = \frac{108}{15} - \frac{56}{15} = \frac{52}{15} = 3\frac{7}{15}\right)$.

29 **320 cm²** To find the area of a rectangle, multiply the length by the width. The length is 8 + 4 + 8 = 20; the width is 6 + 4 + 6 = 16; 20 × 16 = 320 cm².

30 **128 cm²** Divide the cross into 3 rectangles. Find the area of each and add them together (area 1 = 4 cm × 6 cm = 24 cm²; area 2 = 20 cm × 4 cm = 80 cm²; area 3 = 4 cm × 6 cm = 24 cm²; 24 cm + 80 cm + 24 cm = 128 cm²).

31 **192 cm²** Subtract the area of the cross from the total area of the flag (320 cm² – 128 cm² = 192 cm²).

32 **72 cm** The perimeter of a rectangle can be found by adding up the 2 lengths and the 2 widths (20 + 16 + 20 + 16 = 72 cm).

33 **72 cm** The perimeter of the cross can be found by adding the length of each side (4 + 6 + 8 + 4 + 8 + 6 + 4 + 6 + 8 + 4 + 8 + 6 = 72 cm)

34–37 An acute angle is less than 90°. A right angle is exactly 90°. An obtuse angles is greater than 90° but less than 180°. A reflex angle is greater than 180°.

34 **obtuse angle**   35 **right angle**

36 **acute angle**   37 **reflex angle**

38–41 The pattern here is that each triangle has the same number of dots as the number of the triangle squares, so the first triangle has 1 dot (1² = 1), the second triangle has 4 dots (2² = 4) and so on.

38 **25** The fifth triangle will have 25 dots because 5² = 25.

39 **49** The seventh triangle will have 49 dots because 7² = 49.

40 **121** The eleventh triangle will have 121 dots because 11² = 121.

41 **400** The twentieth triangle will have 400 dots because 20² = 400.

42 **10 kg of carrots** 1 kg ≈ 2.2 lb

43 **14 km** 1 mile ≈ 1.6 km

44 **2 pints** 1 litre ≈ 1.75 pints

45 **2040m** Only count the space *between* each post; 24 × 85 = 2040 m

46 **£37 800** To find 5% of a number, find 10% (by dividing by 10) and then halve the result (£36 000 ÷ 10 = £3600; £3600 ÷ 2 = £1800). This gives the increase, which can be added to the original salary to find the new salary (£36 000 + £1800 = £37 800).

47 **19** The cricketer has scored an average of 12 runs in 6 innings. So in the 6 innings his total number of runs was 6 × 12 = 72. For an average of 13 runs in 7 innings, the cricketer would need a total number of runs of 7 × 13 = 91. So in the seventh inning he needs 91 – 72 = 19 runs.

48 **148.29** Adjust the numbers so that they have an equal amount of digits: 4.50 is the same as 4.500; 16.7 is the same as 16.70

		4	·	5	0
	1	6	·	7	0
1	2	7	·	0	9
1	4	8	·	2	9
	1	1			

49–50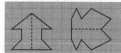

Paper 8 (pages 19–21)

1 **97 kg** There are 1000 kg in 1 tonne so 0.225 tonnes × 1000 = 225 kg; 225 kg – 128 kg = 97 kg

2 **2** $a = 2$ so $4a = 4 \times 2 = 8$; $b = 3$ so $2b = 2 \times 3 = 6$; 8 – 6 = 2

3 **27** 1000 ÷ 38 = 26.32; round up to the next complete page.

4–7 In 24-hour time, 0:00–11:59 represent the times from midnight to midday (a.m.) and 12:01–23:59 represent the times from midday to midnight (p.m.). To change from 24-hour to 12-hour time, if the time begins with a number between 1 and 11, write 'a.m' after the time. If the time begins with a number between

13 and 23, subtract 12 from it to get the new time. If the time begins with 00, then it is 12am; if it begins with 12, then it is 12pm.

4 **10:10**   **5** **23:20**   **6** **01:01**   **7** **19:45**

8–22 A face is a flat surface of a 3D shape, an edge is a straight line where two faces meet and a vertex is a corner where three or more faces meet.

Name of solid	Faces	Vertices	Edges
Triangular prism	5	6	9
Square prism	6	8	12
Triangular-based pyramid	4	4	6
Square-based pyramid	5	5	8
Cube	6	8	12

23 **36 minutes** To find the time Mrs Forgetmenot arrives at the station, add 9 minutes to 9:42 (9:42 + 9 minutes = 9:51). Subtract this time from 10:27 to find how long she has to wait (10:27 – 9:51 = 36 minutes)

24–28 To write one number as a percentage of another, write them as a fraction. Here the number who took part is the numerator and the number of members is the denominator. Then rewrite the fraction as an equivalent fraction with a denominator of 100.

24 **79%** $\frac{79}{100} = 79\%$ **25** **72%** $\frac{36}{50} = \frac{72}{100} = 72\%$

26 **80%** $\frac{120}{150} = \frac{40}{50} = \frac{40}{100} = 80\%$

27 **70%** $\frac{49}{70} = \frac{7}{10} = \frac{70}{100} = 70\%$

28 **75%** $\frac{60}{80} = \frac{3}{4} = \frac{75}{100} = 75\%$

29 **2** $x = 5$ so $4x = 4 \times 5 = 20$; $y = 2$ so $5y = 5 \times 2 = 10$; $20 \div 10 = 2$

30–40 Start with the time given and subtract to work out the other times. For example, if the fifth lesson ends at 12:25 and each lesson lasts for 30 minutes, then it begins at 11:55. The time a lesson ends is the same time as the start of the next lesson.

	Begins	Ends
1st lesson	9:40	10:10
2nd lesson	10:10	10:40
3rd lesson	10:40	11:10
Break	11:10	11:25
4th lesson	11:25	11:55
5th lesson	11:55	12:25

41 **9** $2475 \div 25 = 99$; $99 \div 11 = 9$

42–43 **3, 11** of 2475, divide by 5 first. $2475 \div 5 = 495$; $495 \div 5 = 99$; $99 \div 3 = 33$; $33 \div 3 = 11$. The prime factors of 2475 are 3 and 5 and 11.

44 **32.25** If 10.75 krone is equal to £1, multiply both numbers by 3 to find out how many krone there are for £3 ($10.75 \times 3 = 32.25$).

45 **12.81** If 8.54 krone is equal to £1, multiply both numbers by 1.5 to find out how many krone there are for £1.50 ($8.54 \times 1.5 = 12.81$).

46 **14.95** If €1.15 is equal to £1, multiply both numbers by 13 to find out how many euros there are for £13 ($1.15 \times 13 = 14.95$).

47 **86.00** If $1.72 is equal to £1, multiply both numbers by 50 to find out how many dollars there are for £50 ($1.72 \times 50 = 86$).

48–49 To solve a ratio, add up the ratio numbers (6 + 7 = 13). Then divide this number into the number of children ($351 \div 13 = 27$). Finally, multiply this number by the individual ratios.

48 **189** $7 \times 27 = 189$ **49** **162** $6 \times 27 = 162$

50 **11** To complete this type of question, work backwards through the equation: $242 \div 2 = 121$; $11 \times 11 = 121$

Paper 9 (pages 22–24)

1 **parallelogram** It has 2 sets of parallel lines; 2 longer and 2 shorter sides, 1 pair are diagonal.

2 **trapezium** The shape has 1 set of parallel lines; 1 shorter and 1 longer.

3 **rhombus** The shape has 2 sets of parallel lines; all 4 lines the same length, 1 pair are diagonal.

4 **rectangle** The shape has 2 sets of parallel lines; 2 longer and 2 shorter sides.

5 **kite** The shape has 2 shorter and 2 longer sides.

6 **Singapore** With a temperature of 31° C, Singapore was hottest.

7 **Montreal** With a temperature of –10° C, Montreal was coldest.

8 **30 °C** 27 °C – –3 °C = 27 °C + 3 °C = 30 °C

9 **31° C** 26 °C – –5 °C = 26 °C + 5 °C = 31 °C

10 **41° C** 31 °C – –10 °C = 31 °C + 10 °C = 41 °C

11 **7353** 9732 – 2379 = 7353

12 **8** 1500p ÷ 175p = 8.571; round down to the nearest whole number to find the number of comics.

13 **123** $6027 \div 7 = 861$, so $y = 861$; $861 \div 7 = 123$

14–23 First work out the sequence between the numbers. Then use the same rule to find the next two numbers.

14–15 $6\frac{1}{2}$, $7\frac{1}{4}$ The sequence is to add $\frac{3}{4}$; $5\frac{3}{4} + \frac{3}{4} = 6\frac{1}{2}$; $6\frac{1}{2} + \frac{3}{4} = 7\frac{1}{4}$

16–17 **66, 60** The sequence is to take away 10, then take away 9, then take away 8, and so on; $73 – 7 = 66$; $66 – 6 = 60$.

18–19 **73, 82** The sequence is to add 5, then add 6, then add 7, and so on; $65 + 8 = 73$; $73 + 9 = 82$

20–21 **32, 47** The sequence is to add 3, then add 6, then add 9, and so on; 20 + 12 = 32; 32 + 15 = 47

22–23 **32, 64** The sequence is to multiply by 2; 16 × 2 = 32; 32 × 2 = 64

24–25 **18 cm, 6 cm** Use a to represent the width of the rectangular piece of paper. The length is 3 times the width, or $3a$. So the perimeter is $a + 3a + a + 3a = 8a$. The perimeter is 48 cm so a is 48 ÷ 8 = 6 cm. The width is a so the width is 6 cm. The length is $3a$, so the length is 6 cm × 3 = 18 cm.

26–30

You start facing	turn through	clockwise /anticlockwise	you are now facing
W	135°	anticlockwise	SE
SE	45°	clockwise	S
NE	90°	anticlockwise	NW
SW	45°	anticlockwise	S
S	180°	clockwise	N

31 **£0.40 or 40p** £1.70 – £1.30 = £0.40
32 **£0.20 or 20p** £0.40 ÷ 2 = £0.20
33 **£0.90 or 90p** £1.30 – £0.40 = £0.90
34 **£0.30 or 30p** £0.90 ÷ 3 = £0.30
35 **0.385**

H	T	U	·	t	h	th
3	8	5				
		0	·	3	8	5

36 **0.000 12**

U	·	t	h	th	tth	hth
0	·	1	2			
0	·	0	0	0	1	2

37 **0.0078**

U	·	t	h	th	hth
7	·	8			
0	·	0	0	7	8

38 **0.049**

T	U	·	t	h	th
4	9				
	0	·	0	4	9

39 **2789** Subtract the number of men and children from the total population; 11 552 – 8763 = 2789

40 **5678** Subtract the number of men and women from the total population; 11 552 – 5874 = 5678

41 **3085** Subtract the number of women and the number of children from the total population; 11 552 – 2789 – 5678 = 3085

42 **3, 4, 6, 12** 1 × 12 = 12, 2 × 6 = 12, 3 × 4 = 12
43 **2, 4, 5, 10, 20** 1 × 20 = 20, 2 × 10 = 20, 4 × 5 = 20
44 **1, 3, 5, 15** 1 × 15 = 15, 3 × 5 = 15
45 **2, 4** **46** **3** **47** **5**

48–50 1, 2 and 4 are factors of both 12 and 20, so the width of the box must be 1 cm, 2 cm or 4 cm. 1 and 3 are factors of both 12 and 15, so the height of the box must be 1 cm or 3 cm. 1 and 5 are factors of both 20 and 15, so the length of the box must be 1 cm or 5 cm. The right face of the cube has area of 15 cm², so the height must be 3 cm and the length 5 cm (3 × 5 = 15). The top face of the box has area of 20 cm²; the length is 5 cm, so the width must be 4 cm (5 × 4 = 20).

Paper 10 (pages 24–27)

1–7 If a shape has a line of symmetry, the sides on either side of the line will be identical.

1 H **2–5** B, D, E, G **6** A **7** C

8 **4 hours** If it takes 8 people 10 hours, it will take 1 person 8 × 10 = 80 hours. So it will take 20 people 80 ÷ 20 = 4 hours

9–11 To find the mean of a set of numbers, add the numbers together and then divide the total by the quantity of numbers in the group.

9 **7** 7 + 11 + 4 + 6 = 28; 28 ÷ 4 = 7
10 **4** 7 + 1 + 4 + 6 + 2 = 20; 20 ÷ 5 = 4
11 **7** 7 + 11 + 4 + 6 + 2 + 12 = 42; 42 ÷ 6 = 7
12 **45 m** 1.575 km = 1.575 × 1000 = 1575 m; 1575 m ÷ 35 = 45 m. Only count the space *between* each post.

13–19 To find the profit, subtract the wholesale price from the retail price. To find the wholesale price, subtract the profit from the retail price. To find the retail price, add the profit to the wholesale price.

Wholesale price (Price at the factory)	Retail price (Price in the shop)	Profit (Money made by shopkeeper)
£7.85	£9.22	**£1.37**
£14.76	£17.10	£2.34
£38.75	**£44.42**	£5.67
£17.37	£21.14	**£3.77**
£41.85	**£50.04**	£8.19
£54.89	£67.76	£12.87
£0.87	**£1.05**	£0.18

20–24 When plotting coordinates on a gird, use the rule "along the corridor and up the stairs" to remember to go horizontal, then vertical.

A10

25 M

26–28 £4, £3.50, £2.50 To solve a ratio, add up the ratio numbers (8 + 7 + 5 = 20). Then divide this number into the total sum of money (£10.00 ÷ 20 = 50p). Finally, multiply this answer by the individual ratios (Emma gets 8 × 50p = £4; Salim gets 7 × 50p = £3.50; Katie gets 5 × 50p = £2.50).

29 625 There are 1000 grams in a kilogram; 1000 g – 375 g = 625 g.

30 124 There are 1000 grams in a kilogram; 3000 ÷ 125 g = 24 packets.

31–36 First write each decimal as a mixed number. Then reduce the fraction to its simplest form

31 $3\frac{4}{5}$ $3.8 = 3\frac{8}{10} = 3\frac{4}{5}$

32 $11\frac{2}{5}$ $11.4 = 11\frac{4}{10} = 11\frac{2}{5}$

33 $11\frac{1}{500}$ $11.002 = 11\frac{2}{1000} = 11\frac{1}{500}$

34 $3\frac{1}{4}$ $3.25 = 3\frac{25}{100} = 3\frac{1}{4}$

35 $6\frac{1}{2}$ $6.5 = 6\frac{5}{10} = 6\frac{1}{2}$

36 $1\frac{3}{25}$ $1.12 = 1\frac{12}{100} = 1\frac{6}{50} = 1\frac{3}{25}$

37 £9.00 Use a to represent the cost of child ticket. Therefore $2a$ represents the cost of an adult ticket. $2a + 2a + a + a + a = £31.50$ so $7a = £31.50$; $a = £31.50 ÷ 7 = £4.50$. So an adult ticket costs $£4.50 × 2 = £9.00$.

38–43 To find a time interval, subtract the later time from the earlier time.

38 B A takes 07:04 – 06:15 = 49 minutes; B takes 08:21 – 07:33 = 48 minutes

39 C C takes 20:48 – 19:57 = 51 minutes; D takes 22:10 – 21:23 = 47 minutes

40 11 hours 36 minutes 19:57 – 08:21 = 11 hours 36 minutes

41 20:19

42 1 hour 36 minutes 49 minutes + 47 minutes = 1 hour 36 minutes

43 20:32

44–46 First, work out 20% of the prices provided. An easy way to do this is to work out 10% (by dividing by 10) and then doubling the result. This gives the reduction, which can be subtracted from the 'Ordinary price' to give the 'Sale price'.

44 £16 10% of £20.00 is £2.00; £2.00 × 2 = £4.00; £20.00 – £4.00 = £16.00

45 £28 10% of £35.00 is £3.50; £3.50 × 2 = £7.00; £35.00 – £7.00 = £28.00

46 £48 10% of £60.00 is £6.00; £6.00 × 2 = £12.00; £60.00 – £12.00 = £48.00

47–50 A horizontal line goes from left to right. A vertical line goes from top to bottom. Parallel lines are the same distance away from each other, all along their length. Perpendicular lines meet at a right angle.

47 FALSE 48 TRUE 49 TRUE 50 TRUE

1 Line B The cyclist took longer to travel a shorter distance.

2 20 9am – 12pm is 3 hours. The cyclist travels 60km, so 60 ÷ 3 = 20km/h

3 50 Between 10.30 and 11.30 (1 hour) the motorist traveled 50km and the line stays at the same rate, so 50 ÷ 1 = 50

4 10:30 a.m.   **5 9 a.m.**

6 11:30 a.m. Line A crosses Line B at 11:30 a.m.

7 50 km

8 £65 Round £4.98 to £5: 13 × £5 = £65

9 15 The average of the 4 numbers is $10\frac{1}{2}$, so the total of the 4 numbers is $4 × 10\frac{1}{2} = 42$. The average of 3 of the numbers is 9, so the total of these 3 numbers is $3 × 9 = 27$. So the fourth number is $42 – 27 = 15$.

10–14 $\frac{3}{8}, \frac{1}{2}, \frac{2}{3}, \frac{3}{4}, \frac{5}{6}$ First find equivalent fractions so that the bottom numbers (the denominators) are all the same. Then compare the top numbers (numerators). $\frac{1}{2} = \frac{12}{24}, \frac{2}{3} = \frac{16}{24}, \frac{5}{6} = \frac{20}{24},$ $\frac{3}{8} = \frac{9}{24}, \frac{3}{4} = \frac{18}{24}.$ So $\frac{9}{24} < \frac{12}{24} < \frac{16}{24} < \frac{18}{24} < \frac{20}{24}$ or $\frac{3}{8} < \frac{1}{2} < \frac{2}{3} < \frac{3}{4} < \frac{5}{6}$

15–17 40, 50, 35 Add up all the numbers in each circle in the Venn diagram. 18 + 9 + 7 + 6 = 40 children like soul, 29 + 9 + 7 + 5 = 50 children like rock and 17 + 6 + 7 + 5 = 35 children like pop music.

18 16 Add the numbers in the overlap between the circle for soul and the circle for rock (9 + 7 = 16).

19 13 Add the numbers in the overlap between the circle for soul and the circle for pop (6 + 7 = 13).

20 none Cube A has 2 light grey sides so it cannot be a match. Both Cube B and Cube C have one face that is black, so they cannot be correct either.

21 A Cube A has 2 light grey sides and 1 dark grey side.

22 B Cube A has 2 light grey sides so it cannot be a match. Cube C has 1 side with a grid pattern, so it cannot be a match either.

23 none Cube A has 2 light grey sides so it cannot be a match. Cube B has 1 side with a wave pattern so it cannot be a match. In the net the light grey side and the black side are in opposite positions, so they cannot be adjacent as they are in cube C.

24 C Cube A has 2 light grey sides so it cannot be a match. Cube B has a 1 side with a wave pattern so it cannot be a match.

25 $\frac{3}{8}$ $\left(\frac{1}{4} = \frac{2}{8}$ and $\frac{1}{8} + \frac{2}{8} = \frac{3}{8}\right)$.

26 **0.23** 2.00 – 1.77 = 0.23

27 **0.09** 3 × 3 = 9. There are 2 numbers after the decimal points in the question, so there must be 2 numbers after the decimal point in the answer (0.3 × 0.3 = 0.09).

28 **5** 3 ÷ 0.6 is the same as 30 ÷ 6 = 5.

29–33 When plotting coordinates on a grid, use the rule "along the corridor and up the stairs" to remember to go horizontal, then vertical.

34–35 **(–3, 3)**   36–37 **(–1, 1)**

38–40 To multiply by 100, place the numbers in a decimal grid (using hundreds, tens, units, tenths, hundredths, thousandths, etc.) Increase a number by 100 by moving it 2 places to the left.

38 **2620**

Th	H	T	U	·	t
		2	6	·	2
2	6	2	0		

39 **890**

H	T	U	·	t
		8	·	9
8	9	0		

40 **2516**

Th	H	T	U	·	t	h
		2	5	·	1	6
2	5	1	6	·		

41–43 **84, 42, 21** For every 1p coin, there are 2 2p coins with a value of 2 × 2 = 4p and 4 5p coins with a value of 4 × 5 = 20p. This gives the ratio 1 : 4 : 20. To solve a ratio, add up the ratio numbers (1 + 4 + 20 = 25). Then divide this number into the total value of the coins in pence (525 ÷ 25 = 21). Multiply this number by the individual ratios to find the value of each type of coin (there is 1 × 21 = 21p in 1p coins, 4 × 21 = 84p in 2p coins and 20 × 21 = 420p in 5p coins). Finally, divide the values by the coin values to find the number of coins of each type (21p × 1p = 21 1p coins, 84p ÷ 2p = 42 2p coins and 420p ÷ 5p = 84 5p coins).

44–46 **60, 30, 15** If Tom was 1 year old, Uncle John would be 2 years old and Grandma would be 4 years old. This gives the ratio 1 : 2 : 4. To solve a ratio, add up the ratio numbers (1 + 2 + 4 = 7). The divide this number into the total of their ages (105 ÷ 7 = 15). Finally, multiply this number by the

individual ratios to find the ages (Tom is 1 × 15 = 15 years old, Uncle John is 2 × 15 = 30 years old and Grandma is 4 × 15 = 60 years old).

47–50 To divide by 1000, place the numbers in a decimal grid, using hundreds, tens, units, tenths, hundredths, thousandths, etc. Reduce a number by 1000 by moving it 3 places to the right.

47 **0.0342**

T	U	·	t	h	th	tth
3	4	·	2			
	0	·	0	3	4	2

48 **0.0086**

U	·	t	h	th	tth
8	·	6			
0	·	0	0	8	6

49 **0.2746**

H	T	U	·	t	h	th	tth
2	7	4	·	6			
		0	·	2	7	4	6

50 **0.003**

U	·	t	h	th
3				
0	·	0	0	3

Paper 12 (pages 31–33)

1–5 The function machine multiplies each number by 10 and then subtracts 3.

1 **337** 34 × 10 = 340; 340 – 3 = 337

2 **427** 43 × 10 = 430; 430 – 3 = 427

3 **517** 52 × 10 = 520; 520 – 3 = 517

4 **607** 61 × 10 = 610; 610 – 3 = 607

5 **697** 70 × 10 = 700; 700 – 3 = 697

6 **10^4** 7 **7^3** 8 **5^5** 9 **1^6** 10 **4^4** 11 **11^5** 12 **1**

13 **63 m²** The area of a rectangle can be found by multiplying the length by the width (9 × 7 = 63).

14 **32 m** The perimeter of a rectangle can be found by adding up the 2 lengths and the 2 widths (9 + 7 + 9 + 7 = 32 m).

15–17 Find the equivalent cost for 1 kg at each size. There are 1000 grams in a kilogram. A: 1 kg costs £3.81; B 1000 g ÷ 200 g = 5, so 1 kg costs 5 × £1.10 = £5.50; C 1000 g ÷ 125 g = 8, so 1 kg costs 8 × £0.54 = £4.32; D 1000 g ÷ 250 g = 4, so 1 kg costs 4 × £0.93 = £3.72; E 1000 g ÷ 750 g = $1\frac{1}{3}$, so 1 kg costs $1\frac{1}{3}$ × £3.97 = £5.29; F 1000 g ÷ 400 g = 2.5, so 1 kg costs 2.5 × £1.56 = £3.90

15 **D** With a cost of £3.72 per kilogram, Tin D was the best bargain.

16 **A** With a cost of £3.81 per kilogram, Tin A was the second best bargain.

17 **F** With a cost of £3.90 per kilogram, Tin F was the third best bargain.

18–20 There are 5 increments between 0.80 and 0.81. Take the difference between these numbers (0.81 – 0.80 = 0.01) and divide it by the number of increments (0.01 ÷ 5 = 0.002). Then label each increment (e.g. 0.812, 0.814, 0.816, 0.818).

18 **0.822**   19 **0.806**   20 **0.798**

21 **6** Pavel's temperature was above normal on the first Monday, the first Tuesday, Wednesday, Thursday, Friday and Saturday.

22 **1** Pavel's temperature was below normal on the second Monday.

23 **Tuesday** Pavel's temperature was highest on the first Tuesday.

24 **Thursday** Pavel's temperature began to fall on the Thursday (and did not increase again).

25 **98.4 °F** There are 10 increments between 98 and 99. Take the difference between these numbers (99 – 98 = 1) and divide it by the number of increments (1 ÷ 10 = 0.1). So each small square on the temperature axis represents 0.1 °F.

26–31 To solve this type of question, make all the fractions equivalent. Here, use denominators of 100 (Mathematics $\frac{54}{75} = \frac{18}{25} = \frac{72}{100}$; English $\frac{48}{60} = \frac{16}{20} = \frac{80}{100}$; History $\frac{27}{40} = \frac{13.5}{20} = \frac{67.5}{100}$, French $\frac{25}{40} = \frac{12.5}{20} = \frac{62.5}{100}$; Geography $\frac{39}{50} = \frac{78}{100}$; Art $\frac{15}{20} = \frac{75}{100}$) and then order them ($\frac{80}{100}$ (English) > $\frac{78}{100}$ (Geography) > $\frac{75}{100}$ (Art) > $\frac{72}{100}$ (Mathematics) > $\frac{67.5}{100}$ (History) > $\frac{62.5}{100}$ (French)).

26 **English**   27 **Geography**   28 **Art**
29 **Mathematics**   30 **History**   31 **French**

32–41 First work out the sequence between the numbers. Then use the same rule to find the next two numbers.

32–33 **22, 27** The sequence is to add 1, then add 2, then add 3, and so on; so 18 + 4 = 22 and 22 + 5 = 27.

34–35 **0.5, 0.05** The sequence is to divide by 10; 5 ÷ 10 = 0.5 and 0.5 ÷ 10 = 0.05.

36–37 $4\frac{1}{2}, 8\frac{1}{2}$ The amount added each time is doubled: $\frac{1}{4}$ is added, then $\frac{1}{2}$, then 1, then 2, then 4.

38–39 **1.0, 1.1** The rule is to add 0.1; 0.9 + 0.1 = 1.0; 1.0 + 0.1 = 1.1

40–41 **0.625, 0.75** The rule is to add 0.125; 0.5 + 0.125 = 0.625; 0.625 + 0.125 = 0.75

42–43 **16, 17** The mode is the most common score. Two people scored 16 and two people scored 17.

44 **17** To find the median of a set of numbers, list the numbers in order, smallest to largest (16, 16, 17, 17, 18). The median is the middle value.

45 **2** The range is the difference between the highest score and the lowest score (18 – 16 = 2).

46 **16.8** To find the mean of a set of numbers, add the numbers together and then divide the total by the quantity of numbers in the group (17 + 16 + 18 + 16 + 17 = 84; 84 ÷ 5 = 16.8).

47 **16** The modes is the most common score. Three people now scored 16.

48 **16** To find the median of a set of numbers, list the numbers in order, smallest to largest (16, 16, 16, 17, 18). The median is the middle value.

49 **2** The range is the difference between the highest score and the lowest score (18 – 16 = 2).

50 **16.6** To find the mean of a set of numbers, add the numbers together and then divide the total by the quantity of numbers in the group (16 + 16 + 18 + 16 + 17 = 83; 83 ÷ 5 = 16.6).

Paper 13 (pages 34–36)

1–3
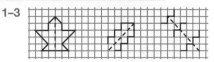

4 $\frac{2}{5}$ $\frac{1}{5} = \frac{2}{10}$; $\frac{2}{10} + \frac{2}{10} = \frac{4}{10}$; $\frac{4}{10} = \frac{2}{5}$.

5 **0.07** 0.49 ÷ 7 = 0.07

6 **7** To find 20% of a number, first find 10% (by dividing by 10) and then double the result (10% of 35 = 3.5; 3.5 × 2 = 7)

7 **7** $4^2 = 4 \times 4 = 16$; $3^2 = 3 \times 3$) = 9; 16 – 9 = 7

8 **4** $2^3 = 2 \times 2 \times 2 = 8$; $2^2 = 2 \times 2 = 4$; 8 – 4 = 4

9 **25 cm** There are 100 centimetres in 1 metre. 25% is the same as $\frac{1}{4}$. $\frac{1}{4}$ of 100 cm = 100 cm ÷ 4 = 25 cm.

10 **0.001** 1 × 1 × 1 = 1. There are 3 numbers after the decimal points in the question, so there must be 3 numbers after the decimal point in the answer (0.1 × 0.1 × 0.1 = 0.001).

11 $\frac{1}{2}$ $\frac{1}{3} = \frac{2}{6}$; $\frac{2}{6} + \frac{1}{6} = \frac{3}{6}$; $\frac{3}{6} = \frac{1}{2}$.

12–14 **£2, £1, £0.40 or 40p** For every 10p Angela gets, May gets 5p and Claire gets 2p. To solve a ratio, add up the ratio numbers (10 + 5 + 2 = 17). Then divide this number into the total amount of money (£3.40 ÷ 17 = £0.20). Finally, multiply this number by the individual ratios (Angela get 10p × £0.20 = £2; Maya gets 5p × £0.20 = £1; Claire gets 2p × £0.20 = £0.40).

15 **£0.80 or 80p** $\frac{3}{4}$ of the sum of money is £1.80. Divide by 3 to find $\frac{1}{4}$ (£1.80 ÷ 3 = £0.60), multiply by 4 to find the whole (£0.60 × 4 = £2.40) and finally divide by 3 to find $\frac{1}{3}$ (£2.40 ÷ 3 = £0.80 or 80p).

16 **9.99** When multiplying decimals, remove the decimal point and multiply the numbers. (3.7 × 3.7 becomes 37 × 37 = 1369) Then

Bond Maths Assessment Papers 10–11+ years Book 1

count the amount of numbers after the decimal point in the question: there are 2 numbers after the decimal points in the question, so there must be 2 numbers after the decimal point in the answer ($3.7 \times 3.7 = 13.69$). $13.69 - 3.7 = 9.99$

17 **6.837** Adjust the numbers so that they have an equal amount of digits: 3.7 is the same as 3.700; 2.95 is the same as 2.950.

	3	·	7	0	0
	2	·	9	5	0
+	0	·	1	8	7
	6	·	8	3	7
		₁		₁	

18 **1.511** Adjust the numbers so that they have an equal amount of digits: 3.2 is the same as 3.200

	²3	·	¹¹2	⁹0	¹0
−	1	·	6	8	9
	1	·	5	1	1

19 **47** $799 \div 17 = 47$

		0	4	7
1	7	7	⁷9	¹¹9

20 **2750**

Th	H	T	U	·	t	h
			2	·	7	5
2	7	5	0			

21 **38 200**

TTh	Th	H	T	U	·	t
			3	8	·	2
3	8	2	0	0		

22 **125**

H	T	U	·	t	h	th
		0	·	1	2	5
1	2	5				

23 **875**

H	T	U	·	t	h	th
		0	·	8	7	5
8	7	5				

24 **30** Add up the bar heights ($2 + 3 + 6 + 12 + 5 + 2 = 30$)

25 **1** 2 children received 91–100 marks. 1 boy gained over 90. So $2 - 1 = 1$.

26 **3** 6 children received 61–70 marks. $\frac{1}{2}$ of them were girls. So $1 - \frac{1}{2} = \frac{1}{2}$ of them were boys; $6 \div 2 = 3$.

27 **1** 2 children received 41–50 marks. $\frac{1}{2}$ of them were boys. So $1 - \frac{1}{2} = \frac{1}{2}$ of them were girls; $2 \div 2 = 1$.

28 **3** 5 children received 81–90 marks. $\frac{2}{5}$ of them were girls. So $1 - \frac{2}{5} = \frac{3}{5}$ of them were boys; $5 \div 5 = 1$; $3 \times 1 = 3$.

29 **3** 12 children received 71–80 marks. $\frac{3}{4}$ of them were boys. So $1 - \frac{3}{4} = \frac{1}{4}$ of them were girls; $12 \div 4 = 3$.

30 **2** 3 children received 51–60 marks. $\frac{1}{3}$ of them were girls. So $1 - \frac{1}{3} = \frac{2}{3}$ of them were boys; $3 \div 3 = 1$; $2 \times 1 = 2$.

31–40 The second column has an 8 and a 12. These are both multiples of 4 so the heading for that column must be 4 and the headings for the first two rows must be 2 ($2 \times 4 = 8$) and 3 ($3 \times 4 = 12$). Use logic to fill in the rest of the table.

×	5	4	9	2
2	10	8	18	4
3	15	12	27	6
7	35	28	63	14
1	5	4	9	2

41–46 To find equivalent fractions, multiply the numerator and the denominator by the same number.

41 **20** $5 \times 5 = 25$; $4 \times 5 = 20$

42 **77** $11 \times 11 = 121$; $7 \times 11 = 77$

43 **56** $8 \times 8 = 64$; $7 \times 8 = 56$

44 **12** $7 \times 6 = 42$; $2 \times 6 = 12$

45 **36** $4 \times 12 = 48$; $3 \times 12 = 36$

46 **49** $9 \times 7 = 63$; $7 \times 7 = 49$

47 **£0.84 or 84p** Divide the total cost by 13 to find the cost of a single item (($£1.56 \div 13 = £0.12$). Then multiply this number by 7 ($£0.12 \times 7 = £0.84$ or 84p).

48–50 **27, 9, 3** For every 1 sweet that Prue has, Ragini has 3 and Penny has 9. This gives the ratio 1 : 3 : 9. To solve a ratio, add up the ratio numbers ($1 + 3 + 9 = 13$). Then divide this number into the number of sweets ($39 \div 13 = 3$). Finally, multiply this number by the individual ratios (Prus has $1 \times 3 = 3$; Ragini has $3 \times 3 = 9$; Penny has $9 \times 3 = 27$).

Paper 14 (pages 36–39)

1–3 $5 \times 12 = 60$ and $12 \times 12 = 144$, so this is the 12 times table.

60	144	72	**132**	120
5	12	**6**	11	**10**

4–6 There are different strategies for solving any of these questions but here is the working out method recommended by the National Curriculum.

4 **4.18**

		0	·	3	8
×				1	1
		3	·	8	0
+		0	·	3	8
		4	·	1	8
				₁	

5 **0.57**

	0	·	5	7
9	5	·	⁵1	⁶3

6 **278**

		9	12	1
	4̶	θ̶	3̶	0̶
−		7	5	2
		2	7	8

7 **10**   8 **5**   9 **5 km**

10 **12 km/h** 2 km in 10 minutes; 6 × 10 minutes = 60 minutes; 2 × 6 = 12 km in 1 hour.

11 **72** 45 × 40 = 1800; 1800 ÷ 25 = 72.

12 **12** 3 + a = 15, a = 15 − 3 = 12

13 **3** x + 4 = 7, so x = 7 − 4 = 3

14 **2** 5 + a = 7, so a = 7 − 5 = 2

15 **16** y − 7 = 9, so y = 9 + 7 = 16

16 **12** b − 4 = 8, so b = 8 + 4 = 12

17 **6** c − 1 = 5, so c = 5 + 1 = 6

18

	1	2	8
7	8	¹9	⁵6

19

	1	3	1
6	7	¹8	6

20

	0	1	3	2
9	1	¹1	²8	¹8

21

	1	2	9
4	5	⁵1	³6

22 **132** The quotient is the result of a division.

23 **4:04 p.m.** 3:45 p.m. + 19 minutes = 4:04 p.m.

24 **216 minutes** 00:00 − 10:29 p.m. = 1 hour 31 minutes = 91 minutes; 2:05 a.m. − 00:00 = 2 hours 5 minutes = 125 minutes; 91 minutes + 125 minutes = 216 minutes.

25 **288** The pie chart is divided into 4 equal sections. Each section represents 72 walkers. So 4 sections represent then 72 × 4 = 288 pupils.

26 **234** The pie chart is divided into 2 equal sections. Each section represents 117 walkers. So 2 sections represent 117 × 2 = 234 pupils.

27 **282** The pie chart is divided into 6 equal sections. Each section represents 47 walkers. So 6 sections represent 47 × 6 = 282 pupils.

28 **264** The pie chart is divided into 8 equal sections. Each section represents 33 walkers. So 8 sections represent 33 × 8 = 264 pupils.

29 **60°** Angles on a straight line add up to 180°; 2x + x = 3x; x = 180° ÷ 3 = 60°.

30 **12°** x = 60°; 2x = 120°

31 **30°** There are 90° in a right-angle; a + a + a = 3a; a = 90° ÷ 3 = 30°.

32 **45°** There are 90° in a right-angle; b + b = 2b; b = 90° ÷ 2 = 45°.

33–43 Start with the time given and subtract to work out the other times. For example, if the fifth lesson ends at 12:50 and each lesson lasts for 40 minutes, then it begins at 12:10. The time a lesson ends is the same time as the start of the next lesson.

	Begins	Ends
1st lesson	**09:15**	**09:55**
2nd lesson	**09:55**	**10:35**
Break	**10:35**	**10:50**
3rd lesson	**10:50**	**11:30**
4th lesson	**11:30**	**12:10**
5th lesson	**12:10**	12:50

44–45 **350, 280** To solve a ratio, add up the ratio numbers (5 + 4 = 9). The divide this number into the number of children (630 ÷ 9 = 70). Finally, multiply this number by the individual ratios (5 × 70 = 350 boys; 4 × 70 = 280 girls).

46–47 **16 cm, 4 cm** Use a to represent the width of the rectangle. The length is 4 times the width, or 4a. So the perimeter is a + 4a + a + 4a = 10a. The perimeter is 40 cm so a is 40 ÷ 10 = 4 cm. The width is a so the width is 4 cm. The length is 4a, so the length is 4 cm × 4 = 16 cm.

48 **5 kg** £6.00 ÷ £1.20 = 5

49 **0.25 kg or 250 g** £1.20 ÷ £0.30 = 4; 1kg ÷ 4 = 0.25 kg or 250 g

50 **£4.20** £1.20 × 3.5 kg = £4.20

Paper 15 (pages 39–42)

1 **26** The mode is the most common score. Two people scored 26.

2 **26** To find the median of a set of numbers, list them in order from smallest to largest (15, 26, 26, 31, 42). The median is the middle number.

3 **27** To find the range of a set of numbers, subtract the smallest value from the largest value (42 − 15 = 27).

4 **28** To find the mean of a set of numbers, add the numbers together and then divide the total by the quantity of numbers in the group (42 + 15 + 26 + 31 + 26 = 140; 140 ÷ 5 = 28).

5 **26** To find the median of a set of numbers, list them in order from smallest to largest (25, 26, 26, 31, 42). The median is the middle number.

6 **17** To find the range of a set of numbers, subtract the smallest value from the largest value (42 − 25 = 17).

7 **£6.00** Multiply £1.20 by 3 to find out how much was left (£3.20 × 3 = £3.60 left), then add on the price of the book (£3.60 + £2.40 = £6.00).

8 **15** Add all the numbers in the oval for the Cycling Club (9 + 6 = 15).

9 **13** Add all the numbers in the oval for the Swimming Club (6 + 7 = 13).

10 **6** This is the number in the overlap of the two ovals.

11 **2** This is the number outside the ovals.

12 **16** Add the numbers that are in the two ovals, but not in the overlap (9 + 7 = 16).

13–18 When reading coordinates, use the rule "along the corridor and up the stairs" to remember to go horizontal, then vertical.

13 **Long Mitton**   14 **Boston**   15 **(1, 4)**

16 **(3, 5)**   17 **20 km**   18 **40 km**

19 **FORWARD 4**   20 **LEFT 90°**   21 **FORWARD 3**

22 **RIGHT 90°**   23 **FORWARD 2**

24–27 Two of the boxes at the end of the tree read "Phone with camera and 3G" and "Phone with no camera, and no 3G". Therefore, the decision tree is sorting phones according to whether they have a camera and whether they have 3G. Use a logical approach to fill in the gaps.

24 **Phone with camera and no 3G**

25 **Phone with no camera, but with 3G**

26 **Does it have 3G?**

27 **Does it have a camera?**

28–30 A horizontal line goes from left to right. A vertical line goes from top to bottom. Parallel lines are the same distance away from each other, all along their length. Perpendicular lines meet at a right angle.

28 **FALSE**   29 **TRUE**   30 **FALSE**   31 **23**

32–33 Halve the number of children by 2 (364 ÷ 2 = 182). Then halve the difference and add half to 182 to find the number of girls, and subtract half from 182 to find the number of boys.

32 **191** 182 girls + 9 = 191

33 **173** 182 boys – 9 = 173

34 **10 989**

		0	^{9}	^{9}	
	1	^{1}4	^{1}0̶	^{1}0̶	^{1}0
–				1	1
	1	0	9	8	9

35–38 The area of a rectangle can be found by multiplying the length by the width. The perimeter of a rectangle can be found by adding up the 2 lengths and the 2 widths. To find the length or width, divide the area by the given dimension.

	Length	Width	Area	Perimeter
Rectangle 1	7 m	4 m	28 m²	22 m
Rectangle 1	9 m	**4 m**	36 m²	**26 m**

39–50 First work out the sequence between the numbers. Then use to same rule to find the next two numbers.

39–40 **47, 65** The sequence is to add 3, then add 6, then add 9 and so on; 32 + 15 = 47; 47 + 18 = 65

41–42 **6.7, 7.2** The sequence is to add 0.1, then add 0.2, then add 0.3 and so on; 6.3 + 0.4 = 6.7; 6.7 + 0.5 = 7.2

43–44 **5, $6\frac{1}{2}$** The sequence is to add $\frac{1}{2}$, then add $\frac{3}{4}$, then add 1 and so on; $3\frac{3}{4} + 1\frac{1}{4} = 5$; $5 + 1\frac{1}{2} = 6\frac{1}{2}$.

45–46 **1, 10** The sequence is to multiply by 10; 0.1 × 10 = 1; 1 × 10 = 10.

47–48 **59, 52** The sequence is to subtract 11, then subtract 10, then subtract 9 and so on; 67 – 8 = 59; 59 – 7 = 52.

49–50 **$\frac{5}{8}, \frac{3}{4}$** The sequence is to add $\frac{1}{8}$; $\frac{1}{2} + \frac{1}{8} = \frac{4}{8} + \frac{1}{8} = \frac{5}{8}$; $\frac{5}{8} + \frac{1}{8} = \frac{6}{8} = \frac{3}{4}$.

Paper 16 (pages 43–45)

1 **75%** $\frac{1}{2}$ of the pupils have one computer and $\frac{1}{4}$ have more than one computer; $\frac{1}{2} + \frac{1}{4} = \frac{3}{4} = 75\%$.

2 **$\frac{1}{4}$**

3 **8** $\frac{1}{4}$ of the pupils have no computer; $32 \times \frac{1}{4} = 32 \div 4 = 8$.

4 **24** $\frac{3}{4}$ of the pupils have at least one computer; $\frac{1}{4} = 8$ so $\frac{3}{4} = 8 \times 3 = 24$.

5 **9** 890 ÷ 31 = 28 r 22; 29 × 31 = 899; 899 – 890 = 9

6 **144** 47 + 48 + 49 = 144

7 **48** To find the mean of a set of numbers, add the numbers together and t hen divide the total by the quantity of numbers in the group (144 ÷ 3 = 48).

8 **2** To find the range of a set of numbers, subtract the smallest number from the largest number (49 – 47 = 2).

9–13 The area of a rectangle can be found by multiplying the length by the width. The perimeter of a rectangle can be found by adding up the 2 lengths and the 2 widths.

9 **1000 m²** 50 m × 20 m = 1000 m²

10 **2800 m²** Length = 10 m + 50 m + 10 m = 70 m; width = 10 m + 20 m + 10 m = 40 m; 70 × 40 = **2800 m²**

11 **1800 m²** 2800 m² – 1000 m² = 1800 m²

12 **140 m** 50 m + 20 m + 50 m + 20 m = 140 m

13 **220 m** 70 m + 40 m + 70 m + 40 m = 220 m

14 **£2.49** Subtract the change from £20 to find how much Jenny spent (£20 – £2.57 = £17.43). Divide by 7 to find the price per metre (£17.43 ÷ 7 = £2.49 per metre).

15 **B** Cube A has 1 light grey side so it cannot be a match. On the net, the dotty face and black face are in opposite positions, so cannot be adjacent, so Cube C cannot be correct either.

16 **A** Cube B has 1 side with a wavy pattern so it cannot be a match. On the net, the dotty face and black face are in opposite positions, so cannot be adjacent, so Cube C cannot be correct either.

17 **none** The net does not fold to make a cube.

18 **C** On the net, the dark grey side and the black side are in opposite positions, so cannot be adjacent, so Cube A cannot be a match. Cube B has 1 side with a wavy pattern, so cannot be correct either.

19 **1** $27 \div 3 = 9$ and $10 - 1 = 9$

20 **14** $20 - 3 = 17$ and $3 + 14 = 17$

21–24 Reduce a number by 1000 by moving it 3 places to the right.

21 **0.0342**

T	U	.	t	h	th	tth
3	4	.	2			
	0	.	0	3	4	2

22 **0.0086**

U	.	t	h	th	tth
8	.	6			
0	.	0	0	8	6

23 **0.2746**

H	T	U	.	t	h	th	tth
2	7	4	.	6			
		0	.	2	7	4	6

24 **0.003**

U	.	t	h	th
3				
0	.	0	0	3

25–27 **72, 36, 18** At the end of the game, for every 1 card that Lewis had, Carl had 2 and Tim had 4. To solve a ratio, add up the ratio numbers $(1 + 2 + 4 = 7)$. Then divide this number into the number of cards $(126 \div 7 = 18)$. Finally, multiply this number by the individual ratios (Lewis had $1 \times 18 = 18$; Carl has $2 \times 18 = 36$; Tim has $4 \times 18 = 72$).

28–30 **75, 31, 20** At the end of the game, Lewis had 18 cards. During the game he lost 2 cards to Tim. So at the beginning of the game he had $18 + 2 = 20$. At the end of the game, Carl had 36 cards. During the game he won 3 cards from Tim and won 2 from Lewis. So at the beginning of the game he had $36 - 3 - 2 = 31$. At the end of the game, Tim had 72 cards. During the game he lost 3 cards to Carl. So at the beginning of the game he had $72 + 3 = 75$

31 **48** Angles on a straight line add up to 180° so the angle for 'Beach' is $180° - 60° = 120°$. There are 360° in a circle so this is $\frac{1}{3}$ of the pie chart. $144 \times \frac{1}{3} = 144 \div 3 = 48$.

32 **24** The angle for 'Sailing' is 60°, which is $\frac{1}{6}$ of the pie chart. $144 \times \frac{1}{6} = 144 \div 6 = 24$.

33 **36** The angle for 'Activity holiday' is 90°, which is $\frac{1}{4}$ of the pie chart. $144 \times \frac{1}{4} = 144 \div 4 = 36$.

34 **18** Angles on a straight line add up to 180° so the angle for 'Camping' is $180° - 90° - 45° = 45°$, which is $\frac{1}{8}$ of the pie chart. $144 \times \frac{1}{8} = 144 \div 8 = 18$.

35 **18** The angle for 'Canal boat' is 45°, which is the same as for 'Camping'.

36–38 **23, 235, 218** Subtract the number of girls and teachers from the total to find the number of boys $(476 - 241 = 235)$. Subtract the number of boys and teachers from the total to find the number of girls $(476 - 258 = 218)$. Subtract the number of boys and the number of girls from the total to find the number of teachers $(476 - 235 - 218 = 23)$.

39 $\frac{1}{2}$ $\frac{1}{3} + \frac{1}{6} = \frac{2}{6} + \frac{1}{6} = \frac{3}{6} = \frac{1}{2}$

40 $\frac{9}{10}$ $\frac{1}{5} = \frac{2}{10}; \frac{2}{10} + \frac{7}{10} = \frac{9}{10}$ 41 **92**

42 **5** $6 \div 1.2$ is the same as $60 \div 12 = 5$.

43 **2** $3^3 = 3 \times 3 \times 3 = 27$; $5^2 = 5 \times 5 = 25$; $27 - 25 = 2$

44 **20**

45 **12** $25\% = \frac{1}{4}$; $\frac{1}{4} \times 48 = 48 \div 4 = 12$

46 $\frac{1}{16}$ To multiply fraction, multiply the numerators and multiply the denominators $(1 \times 1 = 1; 4 \times 4 = 16)$.

47–48 **13, 17**

49–50 **2, 3** A prime factor of a number is a prime number that divides exactly into that number.

Paper 17 (pages 45–47)

1–5 To write one number as a percentage of another, write them as a fraction. Here the actual mark is the numerator and the possible mark is the denominator. Then rewrite the fraction as an equivalent fraction with a denominator of 100.

1 **80%** $\frac{12}{15} = \frac{4}{5} = \frac{80}{100} = 80\%$

2 **60%** $\frac{21}{35} = \frac{3}{5} = \frac{60}{100} = 60\%$

3 **85%** $\frac{68}{80} = \frac{17}{20} = \frac{85}{100} = 85\%$

4 **90%** $\frac{63}{70} = \frac{9}{10} = \frac{90}{100} = 90\%$

5 **70%** $\frac{14}{20} = \frac{70}{100} = 70\%$

6 **33** $12 + 21 = 33$

7 **66%** $\frac{33}{50} = \frac{66}{100} = 60\%$

8–12 Write the percentage as a fraction out of 100, then find an equivalent fraction with the required denominator. The numerator will be Peter's actual mark.

8 **9** $60\% = \frac{60}{100} = \frac{3}{5} = \frac{9}{15}$

9 **28** $80\% = \frac{80}{100} = \frac{4}{5} = \frac{28}{35}$

10 **44** $55\% = \frac{55}{100} = \frac{11}{20} = \frac{44}{80}$

11 **49** $70\% = \frac{70}{100} = \frac{7}{10} = \frac{49}{70}$

12 **13** $65\% = \frac{65}{100} = \frac{13}{20}$

13 **93** $44 + 49 = 93$

14 **62%** $\frac{93}{150} = \frac{31}{50} = \frac{62}{100} = 62\%$

15–18 When rounding a number to the nearest whole number, look at the number in the tenths column. If it is 4 or below, leave the number in the units columns unchanged. If it is 5 or above, raise the number in the units column by 1.

15 **8** The 0.3 in 8.35 rounds down to 8.

16 **1** The 0.7 in 0.71 rounds up to 1.

17 **4** The 0.4 in 4.48 rounds down to 4.

18 **0** The 0.1 in 0.123 rounds down to 0.

19–21 **32, 16, 8** For every 1 bead that Aisha has, Ren has 2 and Sam has 4. To solve a ratio, add up the ratio numbers $(1 + 2 + 4 = 7)$. Then divide this number into the number of beads $(56 ÷ 7 = 8)$. Finally, multiply this number by the individual ratios (Aisha has $1 × 8 = 8$; Ren has $2 × 8 = 16$; Sam has $4 × 8 = 32$).

22 **cube** 23 **triangular-based pyramid**

24 **cuboid** 25 **triangular prism** 26 **30 275**

27 **thirty thousand two hundred and seventy-five**

28–37 To find the length or width or a recangle, given the perimeter, divide the perimeter by 2 and then subtract the given dimension. The area of a rectangle can be found by multiplying the length by the width.

	Length	Width	Perimeter	Area
Rectangle 1	29 m	**1 m**	60 m	**29 m²**
Rectangle 2	28 m	**2 m**	60 m	**56 m²**
Rectangle 3	**25 m**	5 m	60 m	**125 m²**
Rectangle 4	**20 m**	10 m	60 m	**200 m²**
Rectangle 5	15 m	**15 m**	60 m	**225 m²**

38 **2.27** $100 ÷ 2 ÷ 2 = 25$, so multiplying by 100 and then halving and halving again is the same as dividing by 25; $0.0908 × 100 = 9.08$; $9.08 ÷ 2 = 4.54$; $4.54 ÷ 2 = 2.27$.

39–41 1 oz = 25 g, so multiply each of the Imperial measurements by 25 to find the Metric equivalents. The number of eggs will not change.

Ingredient	Imperial	Metric
Plain flour	5 oz	**125 g**
Semolina flour	12 oz	**300 g**
Eggs	11 eggs	**11 eggs**

42 **kilometres** 43 **litres**

44 **tonnes** 45 **millimetres**

46–50 **0.7, 0.707, 0.708, 0.77, 0.78** To order the decimals, looks at the tenths first, then the hundredths and then the thousandths. Remember that 0.7 is the same as 0.70 or 0.700.

Paper 18 (pages 47–50)

1 **22** 19 children have dogs, and 15 children have both dogs and cats, so $19 – 15 = 4$ children have dogs but no cats. 18 children have cats, and 15 children have both dogs and cats, so $18 – 15 = 3$ children have cats but no dogs. The smallest number of children in the class is $15 + 4 + 3 = 22$.

2 **53** $1431 ÷ 27 = 53$.

3 **£4.20** Subtract the cost of the toy from the selling price to find the profit on 1 toy $(£1.60 – £1.25 = £0.35)$. Multiply by 12 to find the total profit on 12 toys $(12 × £0.35 = £4.20)$.

4–15 If $1.14 is equal to £1, multiply both numbers by 10 to find out how many dollars there are for £10. $£10 ÷ £5 = 2$, so divide the result by 2 to find out how many dollars there are for £5. $£5 ÷ £0.50 = 10$, so divide again by 10 to find out how many dollars there are for £0.50. Do the same for the other currencies.

£	US dollars	Indian rupee	Euros	Canadian dollars
£10.00	11.40	932.00	11.20	15.80
£5.00	5.70	466.00	5.60	7.90
£0.50	0.57	46.60	0.56	0.79

16–19 **7.008, 7.088, 7.8, 7.88** To order the decimals, looks at the units first, then the tenths, then the hundredths and then the thousandths. Remember that 7.8 is the same as 7.80 or 0.800.

20–25 Make sure you know the common equivalent fraction, decimals and percentages.

Fraction	Decimal	Percentage
$\frac{1}{2}$	**0.5**	**50%**
$\frac{1}{4}$	0.25	25%
$\frac{1}{5}$	**0.2**	**20%**

26 **7** $56 ÷ a = 8$; $8 × 7 = 56$ so $a = 7$

27 **7** $49 ÷ b = 7$; $7 × 7 = 49$ so $b = 7$

28 **8** $x = 72 ÷ 9 = 8$

29 **12** $y ÷ 4 = 3$; $4 × 3 = 12$ so $y = 12$

30 **63** $z ÷ 9 = 7$; $9 × 7 = 63$ so $z = 63$

31 **3** A product is found by multiplying numbers together. One of the numbers is 37, so divide 111 by 37 to find the other number $(111 ÷ 37 = 3)$.

32–34 To solve a number square, take any complete row and work out the sequence between the numbers. Then use the same sequence to find the missing numbers.

32 **9** In the first row (49, 36, 25) the sequence decreasing square numbers (7^2, 6^2, 5^2). If this sequence is applied to the last row (25, 16, x or 5^2, 4^2, x), x must be 3^2, so the answer is 9.

33 **34.6** In the middle row (30.2, 25.8, 21.4) the sequence is to subtract 4.4. If this sequence is applied to the first row (y, 30.2, 25.8), y must be 4.4 greater than 30.2, so the answer is 34.6.

34 $\frac{1}{4}$ In the middle row $\left(\frac{3}{8}, \frac{1}{2}, \frac{5}{8}\right)$ the sequence is to add $\frac{1}{8}$. If this sequence is applied to the last row, $\left(z, \frac{3}{8}, \frac{1}{2}\right)$, z must be $\frac{1}{8}$ less than $\frac{3}{8}$, so the answer is $\frac{2}{8}$, which can be simplified to $\frac{1}{4}$.

35–36 To find a time interval, subtract the later time from the earlier time.

35 **64 minutes or 1 hour 4 mins** A takes 09:00 – 08:11 = 49 minutes; B takes 10:11 – 09:20 = 51 minutes; C takes 18:09 – 17:05 = 64 minutes; D takes 20:09 –19:17 = 52 minutes.

36 **A** Train A arrives in Bath at 08:45.

37 **38 minutes** 20:09 – 19:31 = 38 minutes

38 **18:09**

39–43 All the places shown are ahead of London. To find the time in one of the other places, add the correct number of hours to the time in London. To find the time in London, subtract the correct number of hours from the time in one of the other places.

39 **10:00 p.m.** 10:00 a.m. + 12 hours = 10:00 p.m.

40 **2:30 p.m.** London + $5\frac{1}{2}$ hours = 2:30 p.m.

41 **1:30 p.m.** 3:30 p.m. – 2 hours = 1:30 p.m.

42 **12:15 p.m.** 1:15 p.m. – 1 hour = 12:15 p.m.

43 **5:30 p.m.** It is $2\frac{1}{2}$ hours later in India than in Kenya. 3:00 p.m. + $2\frac{1}{2}$ = 5:30 p.m.

44 **41 year 8 months** 10 + 9 + 11 + 10 = 40 years; 8 + 6 + 4 + 2 = 20 months; there are 12 months in a year, so 20 months becomes 1 year and 20 – 12 = 8 months.

45–46 **10 years and 5 months** To find the mean of a set of numbers, add the numbers together and then divide the total by the quantity of numbers in the group. Deal with the years and months separately (40 ÷ 4 = 10 years; 20 ÷ 4 = 5 months).

47–50 The perimeter of a rectangle can be found by adding up the 2 lengths and the 2 widths.

47 **56 cm** 20 cm + 8 cm + 20 cm + 8 cm = 56 cm

48 **36 cm** 10 cm + 8 cm + 10 cm + 8 cm = 36 cm

49 **60 cm** 20 cm + 10 cm + 20 cm + 10 cm = 60 cm

50 **127 cm** 56 cm + 36 cm + 35 cm = 127 cm

Paper 19 (pages 50–52)

1–4 Reduce a number by 10 by moving it one place to the right. Then write the digits to the right of the decimal point as a fraction in its lowest terms.

1 $7\frac{4}{5}$ 78 ÷ 10 = 7.8 = $7\frac{8}{10}$ = $7\frac{4}{5}$

2 $47\frac{1}{2}$ 475 ÷ 10 = 47.5 = $47\frac{5}{10}$ = $47\frac{1}{2}$

3 $31\frac{1}{4}$ 312.5 ÷ 10 = 31.25 = $31\frac{25}{100}$ = $31\frac{1}{4}$

4 $\frac{1}{8}$ 1.25 ÷ 10 = 0.125 = $\frac{125}{1000}$ = $\frac{1}{8}$

5 **2650** There are 1000 metres in a kilometre; 4000 m – 1350 m = 2650 m.

6–13 The second row has 56, 16 and 24. These are all multiples of 8 so the heading for that row must be 8 and the headings for the last three columns must be 7 (7 × 8 = 56), 2 (2 × 8 = 6) and 3 (3 × 8 = 24). Use logic to fill in the rest of the table.

×	5	7	2	3
8	**15**	**21**	6	9
8	**40**	56	16	24
4	20	**28**	8	**12**
9	45	63	**18**	**27**

14 **1.7** 10 tenths is 1 and 7 tenths is 0.07

15 **1.43** 100 hundredths is 1, 40 hundredths is 0.4 and 3 hundredths is 0.03

16 **47** 40 units 40 and 7 units is 7

17 **0.007** 7 thousandths is 0.007

18 **2590** 200 tens 2000, 50 tens is 500 and 9 tens is 90

19 **0.14** 10 hundredths is 0.1 and 4 hundredths is 0.04

20–25 Find all the possible answers for the calculation on the right of the equals sign. Then work out how to make one of these possible answers on the left.

20–22 **–, +, –** 5 – 5 + 1 = 1 and 13 – 12 = 1 or **×, ×, +** 5 × 5 × 1 = 13 + 12

23–25 **+, ×, ÷** (3 + 2) × 5 = 25 and 50 ÷ 2 = 25

26 **100** 4.9 × 100 = 490

27 **1.23** 1.23 ÷ 10 = 0.123

28 **13.6** 0.136 × 100 = 13.6

29 **4.4** The average of the 6 numbers is 4. So the total of the 6 numbers is 6 × 4 = 24. If one of the numbers is 2, the total of the remaining 5 numbers is 25 – 2 = 22. So the average of the remaining 5 numbers is 22 ÷ 5 = 4.4.

30–35 First, work out 20% of the prices provided. An easy way to do this is to work out 10% (by dividing by 10) and then doubling the result. This gives the VAT, which can be added to the 'Price before VAT' to give the 'Total price'.

30–31 10% of £530 is £53; £53 × 2 = £106; £530 + £106 = £636

32–33 10% of £165 is £16.50; £16.50 × 2 = £33; £165 + £33 = £198

34–35 10% of £62 is £6.20; £6.20 × 2 = £12.40; £62 + £12.40 = £74.40

Price before VAT	VAT	Total cost
£530	£106	£636
£165	£33	£198
£62	£12.40	£74.40

36–41 The perimeter of a rectangle can be found by adding up the 2 lengths and the 2 widths. To find the length or width, divide the area by the given dimension.

	Length	Width	Perimeter	Area
Piece A	8 cm	3 cm	22 cm	24 cm²
Piece B	6 cm	4 cm	20 cm	24 cm²
Piece C	12 cm	2 cm	28 cm	24 cm²

42–43 Rewrite the fractions as equivalent fraction with a denominator of 100.

42 **50%** $\frac{15}{30} = \frac{5}{10} = \frac{50}{100} = 50\%$

43 **16%** $\frac{4}{25} = \frac{16}{100} = 16\%$ 44 **NO**   45 **YES**

46 **NO**   47 **NO**   48 **NO**   49 **NO**

50 **YES** A parallelogram has 2 pairs of equal, parallel sides.

Paper 20 (pages 52–54)

1–2 **Laser, Spaceship** Subtract Amy's change from £10 to find how much she spent (£10.00 – £4.50 = £5.50). Then find the 2 rides that add up to £5.50.

3–4 **Spaceship, Galaxy** Subtract John's change from £10 to find out how much he spent (£10.00 – £5.65 = £4.35). Then find the 2 rides that add up to £4.35.

5 **£8.60** £1.65 + £1.45 + £2.80 + £2.70 = £8.60

6 **£2.15** To find mean price of a set of numbers, add the numbers together and then divide by the quantity of numbers in the group (£8.60 ÷ 4 = £2.15).

7 **29%** To write one number as a percentage of another, write them as a fraction. Then rewrite the fraction as an equivalent fraction with a denominator of 100 $\left(\frac{58}{200} = \frac{29}{100} = 29\%\right)$.

8–10 **5121, 4021, 8080** Subtract the number of men and women from the total population to find the number of children (17 222 – 9142 = 8080). Subtract the number of women and children from the total population to find the number of men (17 222 – 13 201 = 4021). Subtract the number of men and the number of children

from the total population to find the number of women (17 222 – 8080 – 4021 = 5121).

11 **433** 1000 – 567 = 433

12–14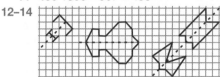

15–20 There are 360° in a circle and 12 hours on a clock. So there are 360° ÷ 12 = 30° between each hour.

15 **6**   16 **1**   17 **4**   18 **2**   19 **5**   20 **3**

21 **51** 4131 ÷ 9 = 459; 459 ÷ 9 = 51

22 **£5.10** 20% = $\frac{20}{100} = \frac{1}{5}$. £2.55 is $\frac{1}{5}$ so $\frac{2}{5}$ is 2 × £2.55 = £5.10

23 **821.5 g** There are 1000 grams in 1 kilogram; 1000 g – 178.5 g = 821.5 g

24 **143** 13 × 11 = 143   25 **225** 15² = 225

26 **8²** 64 = 8 × 8 = 8²   27 **234** 702 ÷ 3 = 234

28 **168** 14 × 12 = 168

29–41 When plotting coordinates on a grid, use the rule "along the corridor and up the stairs" to remember to horizontal, then vertical.

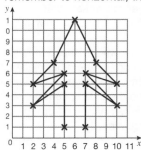

42 **a tree**

43–48 When rounding a number to the nearest 100 000, look at the number in the ten thousands column. If it is 4 or below, leave the number in the hundred thousands column unchanged. If it is 5 or above, raise the number in the hundred thousands column by 1. When rounding a number to the nearest 10 000, look at the number in the thousands column. When rounding a number to the nearest 1 000 000, look at the number in the hundred thousands column.

Ocean	Square km	Square miles
Atlantic	82 200 000	31 700 000
Indian	73 480 000	28 360 000
Pacific	165 000 000	64 000 000

49–50 **70, 490** Divide 560 by 8 to find the number of pupils absent (560 ÷ 8 = 70); take this number away from 560 to find the number of pupils present (560 – 70 = 490).

1–4 An even number × an even number = an even number. An odd number × an odd number = an odd number. An even number × an odd number = an even number.

1 EVEN   2 ODD   3 EVEN   4 EVEN

5–9 When rounding a number to the nearest whole number, look at the number in the tenths column. If it is 4 or below, leave the number in the units column unchanged. If it is 5 or above, raise the number in the units column by 1.

5 £2 The 0.4 in 2.42 rounds down to 2.

6 £3 The 0.7 in 2.71 rounds up to 3.

7 £5 The 0.5 in 4.59 rounds up to 5.

8 £6 The 0.4 in 6.49 rounds down to 6.

9 £8 The 0.5 in 7.50 rounds up to 8.

10 45p Divide 48p by 2 to find $\frac{1}{3}$ of the sum of money, then multiply this by 3 to find the whole (48p ÷ 2 = 24p; 24p × 3 = 72p). Then divide the whole by 8 to find $\frac{1}{8}$, then multiply by 5 to find $\frac{5}{8}$ (72p ÷ 8 = 9p; 9p × 5 = 45p).

11–16 1 kg takes 50 minutes + 20 minutes = 70 minutes = 1 hour 10 minutes. Since each row of the table adds on 0.5 kg, add on 50 ÷ 2 = 25 minutes for each row.

Weight of chicken (kg)	Cooking time
1	1 hour 10 minutes
1.5	1 hour 35 minutes
2	2 hours 0 minutes
2.5	2 hours 25 minutes
3	2 hours 50 minutes
3.5	3 hours 15 minutes

17–19 Reduce a number by 1000 by moving it 3 places to the right.

17 0.374 374 ÷ 1000 = **0.374**

18 0.0148 14.8 ÷ 1000 = **0.0148**

19 0.00255 2.55 ÷ 1000 = **0.00255**

20 189 To find 45% of 420, first find 10% (by dividing by 10) and then multiply the result by 4 to find 40% (420 ÷ 10 = 42; 42 × 4 = 168). Halve 10% to find 5% (42 ÷ 2 = 21). The add the result for 40% and 5% to find 45% (168 + 21 = 189).

21 231 420 − 189 = 231

22–24 To solve a ratio, add up the ratio numbers (8 + 5 + 2 = 15). Then divide this number into the amount of money (£9.00 ÷ 15 = £0.60). Finally, multiply this number by the individual ratios.

22 £4.80 £0.60 × 8 = **£4.80**

23 £3.00 £0.60 × 5 = **£3.00**

24 £1.20 £0.60 × 2 = **£1.20**

25–29 $\frac{5}{6}, \frac{3}{4}, \frac{7}{12}, \frac{11}{24}, \frac{3}{8}$

First find equivalent fractions so that the bottom numbers (the denominators) are all the same. Then compare the top numbers (numerators). $\frac{7}{12} = \frac{14}{24}, \frac{3}{8} = \frac{9}{24}, \frac{3}{4} = \frac{18}{24}, \frac{5}{6} = \frac{20}{24}.$ So $\frac{20}{24} > \frac{18}{24} > \frac{14}{24} > \frac{11}{24} > \frac{9}{24}$ or $\frac{5}{6} > \frac{3}{4} > \frac{7}{12} > \frac{11}{24} > \frac{3}{8}$

30 miles   **31 pints or fluid ounces**

32 ounces   **33 inches** or **feet and inches**

34–37 In 24-hour time, 0:00–11:59 represent the times from midnight to midday (a.m.) and 12:01–23:59 represent the times from midday to midnight (p.m.). To change from 24-hour to 12-hour time, if the time begins with a number between 1 and 11, write 'a.m' after the time. If the time begins with a number between 13 and 23, subtract 12 from it to get the new time. If the time begins with 00, then it is 12am; if it begins with 12, then it is 12pm.

34 08:20 p.m.   **35 08:05 a.m.**

36 12:10 a.m.   **37 05:45 p.m.**

38–39 53, 9 10 + 10 + 11 + 10 + 10 = 51 years; 11 + 8 + 4 + 2 + 8 = 33 months. There are 12 months in year; 33 − 12 − 12 = 9 months and 51 + 2 = 53 years.

40–41 10, 9 To find the average of a set of numbers add the numbers together and then divide the total by the quantity of numbers in the group. 53 years and 9 months does not divide neatly by 5, so repartition 53 years and 9 months as 50 years and 3 × 12 + 9 = 45 months, then deal with the years and months separately (50 ÷ 5 = 10 years; 45 ÷ 5 = 9 months).

42 £1.05 £$\frac{1}{2}$ = 50p, £0.55 = 55p, 27p × 2 = 54p, £$\frac{13}{25}$ = £$\frac{52}{100}$ = 52p, £1.00 − 49p = 51p; 55p + 50p = £1.05

43–45 For every 1 game that Scott has, Anish has 3 and Nick has 6. This gives the ratio 1 : 3 : 6. To solve a ratio, add up the ratio numbers (1 + 3 + 6 = 10). Then divide this number into the number of computer games (140 ÷ 10 = 14). Finally, multiply this number by the individual ratios.

43 14 1 × 14 = 14   **44 42** 3 × 14 = 42

45 84 6 × 14 = 84

46–50 There are 360° in a circle. Here, 360° represents 72 children. 360° ÷ 72 = 5, so 5° represents 1 child.

46 12 A right angle is 90° so the angle for 'Green' is 90° − 30° = 60°; 6 × 2 = 12.

47 33 The angle for 'Blue' is 165°; 16 × 2 + 1 = 32 + 1 = 33.

48 3 Angles on a straight line add up to 180°, so the angle for 'Orange' is 180° − 165° = 15°; 2 + 1 = 3.

49 **9** A right angle is 90°, so the angle for 'Red' is half of 90°, which is 45°; 4 × 2 + 1 = 8 + 1 = 9

50 **6** The angle for 'Pink' is 30°; 3 × 2 = 6.

Paper 22 (pages 57–59)

1–2 Use a to represent the width of the hall. The length is 4 times the width, or $4a$. So the perimeter is $a + 4a + a + 4a = 10a$. The perimeter is 55 m so a is 55 ÷ 10 = 5.5 m.

1 **22 m** The length is $4a$, so the length is 5.5 m × 4 = 22 m.

2 **5.5 m** The width is a so the width is 5.5 m.

3–8 Ahmed has 30 sweets. To find 60%, first find 10% (by dividing by 10), then multiply the result by 6 (30 ÷ 10 = 3; 6 × 3 = 18). So Ahmed as 18 toffees and 30 – 18 = 12 chocolates. Ben has 40 sweets. Divide 40 by 8 to find $\frac{1}{8}$, then multiply by 3 to find $\frac{3}{8}$ (40 ÷ 8 = 5; 3 × 5 = 15). So Ben has 15 chocolates and 40 – 15 = 25 toffees.

3 **Ben** Ahmed has 18 toffees and Ben has 25 toffees.

4–5 **Ahmed, 7** Ben has 25 – 18 = 7 more toffees than Ahmed.

6 **Ben** Ahmed has 12 chocolates and Ben has 15 chocolates.

7–8 **3, Ahmed** Ben has 15 – 12 = 3 more chocolates than Ahmed.

9 **14** The mode is the most popular number. Two people have 14 CDs.

10 **13** To find the median of a set of numbers, put the numbers in order from smallest to largest (5, 8, 12, 14, 14, 19). The median is the middle number. If there are 2 middle numbers, add the 2 numbers together and then divide by 2 (12 + 14 = 26; 26 ÷ 2 = 13).

11 **14** To find the range, subtract the the smallest number from the largest number (19 – 5 = 14).

12 **12** To find the mean of a set of numbers, add the numbers together and then divide the total by the quantity of numbers in the group (8 + 5 + 14 + 19 + 14 + 12 = 72; 72 ÷ 6 = 12).

13 **7 tenths** or $\frac{7}{10}$ 14 **7 units** or **7**

15 **7 tens** or **70**

16 **4230** 3432 is 2000 more than 1432, so 3432 + 798 will be 2000 more than 2230.

17 **4230** 2432 is 1000 more than 1432 and 1798 is 1000 more than 798 so 2432 + 1798 will be 2000 more than 2230.

18 **5230** 4432 is 3000 more than 1432, so 4432 + 798 will be 3000 more than 2230.

19–26 First work out the sequence between the numbers. Then use the same rule to find the next two numbers.

19–20 **77, 75** The sequence is to subtract 6, then subtract 5, then subtract 4 and so on; 80 – 3 = 77; 77 – 2 = 75.

21–22 **53, 49** The sequence is to subtract 12, the subtract 10, then subtract 8 and so on; 59 – 6 = 53; 53 – 4 = 49.

23–24 **45, 51** The sequence is to add 2, then add 3, then add 4 and so on; 40 + 5 = 45; 45 + 6 = 51

25–26 **64, 49** The sequence is decreasing square numbers (12^2, 11^2, 10^2, 9^2); 8^2 = 64; 7^2 = 49.

27–32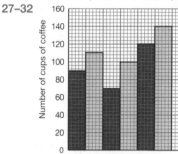

33–37 Subtract each time from the previous time to find how long it takes Train A between stations. Then add these times in turn to 10:05 to build the timetable for Train B.

	Train A arrives at	Train B arrives at
Barwich	07:03	10:05
Hoole	07:48	10:23
Carby	08:02	10:37
Manton	08:15	10:50
Pemby	08:29	11:04
Durwich	08:54	11:29

38–39 **LEFT 90°, FORWARD 1**

40–41 **FORWARD 1, LEFT 90°**

42–43 **RIGHT 90°, FORWARD 2**

44 **125.75 m** 17.5 m × 7 = 122.5 m; 122.5 m + 3.25 m = 125.75 m

45 **56 days** 5th to 31st January = 27 days; there are 28 days in February (2007 is not a leap year); 1st March = 1 day; 27 + 28 + 1 = 56.

46 **£495** 12 × £37.50 = £450; £450 + £45 = £495

47 **64** There are 12 × 5 = 60 fifths in 12; 12 + 4 = 64

48 **120** 6 will divide into 12, so 6 will divide into any number that 12 will divide into. So look for a multiple of 10 that can also be divided by 8 and 12. The lowest number they all divide into is 120.

49 **73** There are 36 houses before number 37 so there must be 36 houses after 37; 36 + 1 + 36 = 73.

50 **6** 5000 ÷ 870 = 5.75; round the answer up to the nearest whole number of stands.

A22

1–10 The first column has 11 and 66. These are both multiples of 11 so the heading for that column must be 11 and the headings for the last two rows must be 1 (1 × 11 = 11) and 6 (6 × 11 = 66). Use logic to fill in the rest of the table.

×	11	9	6	4
8	88	72	48	82
5	55	45	30	20
1	11	9	6	4
6	66	54	36	24

11 71 200 The 40 in 71 246 rounds down to 41 200.

12 1500 The 80 in 1486 rounds up to 1500.

13 1300 The 70 in 1274 rounds up to 1300.

14 700 The 04 in 704.85 rounds down to 700.

15 121 To find a number halfway between two others, add the two numbers together and then divide by 2 (98 + 144 = 242; 242 ÷ 2 = 121).

16–18 12, 177, 205 Subtract the number of teachers and boys from the total to find the number of girls (394 − 189 = 205). Subtract the number of girls and teachers from the total to find the number of boys (394 − 217 = 177). Subtract the number of girls and the number of boys from the total to find the number of teachers (394 − 205 − 177 = 12).

19 143 400 478 × 3 = 1434; 1434 **× 100 = 143 400**

20–23 When a + 3 = 3, a = 0; when a = 1, a + 3 = 1 + 3 = 4; when a + 3 = 5, a = 2; when a = 3, a + 3 = 3 + 3 = 6.

a	0	1	2	3
♣	3	4	5	6

24 17 $9^2 = 81$; $8^2 = 64$; 81 − 64 = 17

25 40 $11^2 = 121$; $9^2 = 81$; 121 − 81 = 40

26 12 $2^3 = 8$; $2^2 = 4$; 8 + 4 = 12

27 9 $5^2 = 25$; $4^2 = 16$; 25 − 16 = 9

28–31 To find the area of a triangle, multiply the height by the length and then divide by 2.

28 15 cm² 6 squares long × 5 squares high = 30 cm²; 30 cm² ÷ 2 = 15 cm²

29 14 cm² 4 squares long × 7 squares high = 28 cm²; 28 cm² ÷ 2 = 14 cm²

30 20 cm² 8 squares long × 5 squares high = 40 cm²; 40 cm² ÷ 2 = 20 cm²

31 15 cm² 5 squares long × 6 squares high = 30 cm²; 30 cm² ÷ 2 = 15 cm²

32–34 There are 365 days in a non-leap year. To divide 365 in the ratio 1 : 4, add up the ratio number (1 + 4 = 5). Then divide this number into the number of days (365 ÷ 5 = 73). Finally, multiply this number by the individual ratios.

32 73 1 × 73 = 73   **33 292** 4 × 73 = 292

34 March 14th January has 31 days and February has 28 days; 73 − 31 − 28 = 14 days in March.

35 48 kg Divide 20 kg by 5 to find $\frac{1}{12}$, then

multiply by 12 to find the whole (20 kg ÷ 5 = 4 kg; 4 kg × 12 = 48 kg).

36 6 kg 48 kg × $\frac{1}{8}$ = 48 kg ÷ 8 = 6 kg.

37–40 Given a, multiply by 3 to find 3a. Given 3a, divide by 3 to find a.

a	2	35	77	47	89
3a	6	105	231	141	267

41 311 The product is the result of multiplying the numbers. The sum is the result of adding the numbers. 27 × 13 = 351; 27 + 13 = 40; 351 − 40 = 311.

42–43 To solve a ratio, add up the ratio numbers (9 + 1 = 10). Then divide this number into the number of sheep (180 ÷ 10 = 18). Finally multiply this number by the individual ratios.

42 162 18 × 9 = 162   **43 18** 18 × 1 = 18

44 £4.70 To divide by a decimal fraction, it is easier to make that number a whole number. Multiply both the decimal fraction and the number you are dividing into by the same number. £7.05 ÷ 1.5 is the same as £14.10 ÷ 3 = £4.70.

45 £16.45 £4.70 × 3.5 = £16.45

46 171 160 ÷ 9 = 17.78, which rounds to 18; 9 × 18 = 162; 162 is not odd, so 162 + 9 = 171

47–50 Deal with the whole numbers and fractions separately. To turn a fraction into a decimal, divide the top number by the bottom number. Then add this to the whole number.

47 3.125 1 ÷ 8 = 0.125   **48 4.05** 1 ÷ 20 = 0.05

49 7.625 1 ÷ 8 = 0.625   **50 9.075** 1 ÷ 40 = 0.075

1 $\frac{7}{12}$ $\left(\frac{1}{3} = \frac{4}{12}, \frac{1}{4} = \frac{3}{12}; \frac{4}{12} + \frac{3}{12} = \frac{7}{12}\right)$.

2 8.01 Adjust the numbers so that they have an equal amount of digits: 10 is the same as 10.00

	9		9		
~~1~~	~~0~~	.	~~0~~	¹0	
	1	.	9	9	
	8	.	0	1	

3 0.016 First work out 4 × 4 = 16. Now count how many digits are after the decimal points in the question (in 0.04 × 0.4 there are 3) and make sure the same number of digits are after the decimal point in the answer. So 0.04 × 0.4 = 0.016.

4 200 4 ÷ 0.02 is the same as 400 ÷ 2 = 200.

5 1.789 Reduce a number by 10 by moving it 1 place to the right.

6 540 2.7 × 2 = 5.4; 5.4 × 100 = 540

7 49 cm² The four sides of a square are the same length, so divide 28 cm by 4 to find the length of 1 side (28 cm ÷ 4 = 7 cm). Multiply the side length by itself to find the area (7 cm × 7 cm = 49 cm²).

8 This is one method.

		1	4	7
	×		4	9
1	3	2	3	
		₄	₆	
5	8	8	0	
	₊	₂		
7	2	0	3	
	₊	₊		

9–15

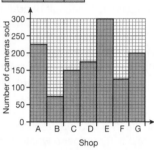

16 **80** First change the metres into cm: 1m = 100cm, so 5m = 500cm and 4m = 400cm. Divide the length and width of the floor by the side length of a tile to find how many tiles will fit along each dimension (500 cm ÷ 50 cm = 10; 400 cm ÷ 50 cm = 8). Multiply the number of tiles that will fit along each dimension to find the number of tiles needed to tile the floor (10 × 8 = 80 tiles).

17 **£60** Divide the number of tiles needed by 10 to find how many set of 10 tiles are needed (80 ÷ 10 = 8). Multiply by £7.50 to find the cost (8 × £7.50 = £60.00).

18–19 **33, 63**

20–23 **1, 3, 7, 21** The factors of a number are the numbers that divide exactly into it (1 × 21 = 21; 3 × 7 = 21).

24–25 **3, 7** The prime factors of a number are the factors that are also prime numbers.

26 **29** 986 ÷ 34 = 29

			0	2	9
3	4	9	⁹8	³⁰6	

27 **£17** Add the 2 amounts of money together and divide by 2 to work out how much Ted and Zac should have if they each have the same amount (£98 + £64 = 162; 162 ÷ 2 = £81). Subtract this from Ted's amount to find how much he must give to Zac (£98 – £81 = £17).

28 **10** The number of children in a class is usually about 30. This is closer to 10 than 100 or 1000.

29 **10 000** The number of people at a Premier League football match will be over 1000 but less than 100 000.

30 **256 cm²** To find the area of a rectangle, multiply the length by the width. In a square, the length and width are the same (16 × 16 = 256 cm²).

31 **112 cm²** Both sides of the flag are divided into 8 sections. 16 ÷ 2 = 8 so each increment represents 2 cm. Divide the cross into 3 rectangles. Find the area of each and add them together (area 1 = 4 cm × 6 cm = 24 cm²; area 2 = 16 cm × 4 cm = 64 cm²; area 3 = 4 cm × 6 cm = 24 cm²; 24 cm + 64 cm + 24 cm = 112 cm²).

32 **144 cm²** Subtract the area of the cross from the total area of the flag (256 cm² – 112 cm² = 144 cm²).

33 **64 cm** The perimeter of a rectangle can be found by adding up the 2 lengths and the 2 widths (16 + 16 + 16 + 16 = 64 cm).

34 **64 cm** The perimeter of the cross can be found by adding the length of each side (4 + 6 + 6 + 4 + 6 + 6 + 4 + 6 + 6 + 4 + 6 + 6 = 64 cm)

35–42 Make sure you know the common equivalent fraction, decimals and percentages.

Fraction	Decimal	Percentage
$\frac{3}{10}$	0.3	30%
$\frac{7}{100}$	0.07	7%
$\frac{1}{4}$	0.25	25%
$\frac{1}{20}$	0.05	5%

43–44 Adjust the numbers so that they have an equal amount of digits: 8 is the same as 8.000 and 2.5 is the same as 2.500.

	⁷		⁹	⁹	
	8	.	θ	θ	¹0
–	1	.	1	2	7
	6	.	8	7	3

		0	1	9	.	0	5
2	5	4	⁴7	²²6	.	¹2	¹²5

43 **6.873** 8.000 – 1.127 = 6.873

44 **19.05** 47.625 ÷ 2.5 is the same as 476.25 ÷ 25 = 19.05.

45–50 To find the profit, subtract the wholesale price from the retail price. To find the wholesale price, subtract the profit from the retail price. To find the retail price, add the profit to the wholesale price.«

Wholesale price	Retail price	Profit
£18.75	£23.50	**£4.75**
£58.85	£70.20	£11.35
£5.13	**£6.10**	97p
£196.50	£235.25	**£38.75**
£11.31	£13.50	£2.19
93p	**£1.12**	19p

A24

44–46 The ages of Grandma, Uncle John and Tom add up to 105 years.

Grandma is twice as old as Uncle John, and Uncle John is twice as old as Tom.

Grandma is _____ years old, Uncle John is _____ years old and Tom
is _____ years old.

Divide each of the following by 1000.

47 34.2 _____

48 8.6 _____

49 274.6 _____

50 3 _____

Now go to the Progress Chart to record your score! **Total** 50

Paper 12

1–5 Write down the numbers that will come out of this machine

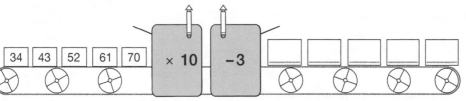

$5 \times 5 = 5^2$ $2 \times 2 \times 2 = 2^3$. Now write the following in the same way.

6 $10 \times 10 \times 10 \times 10 =$ _____

7 $7 \times 7 \times 7 =$ _____

8 $5 \times 5 \times 5 \times 5 \times 5 =$ _____

9 $1 \times 1 \times 1 \times 1 \times 1 \times 1 =$ _____

10 $4 \times 4 \times 4 \times 4 =$ _____

11 $11 \times 11 \times 11 \times 11 \times 11 =$ _____

12 What number is $1 \times 1 \times 1 \times 1 \times 1 \times 1$? _____

13 Find the area of a hall which is 9 metres long and 7 metres wide. _____

14 What is the perimeter of the hall? _____

At the supermarket there were various sizes of *Marvello*.

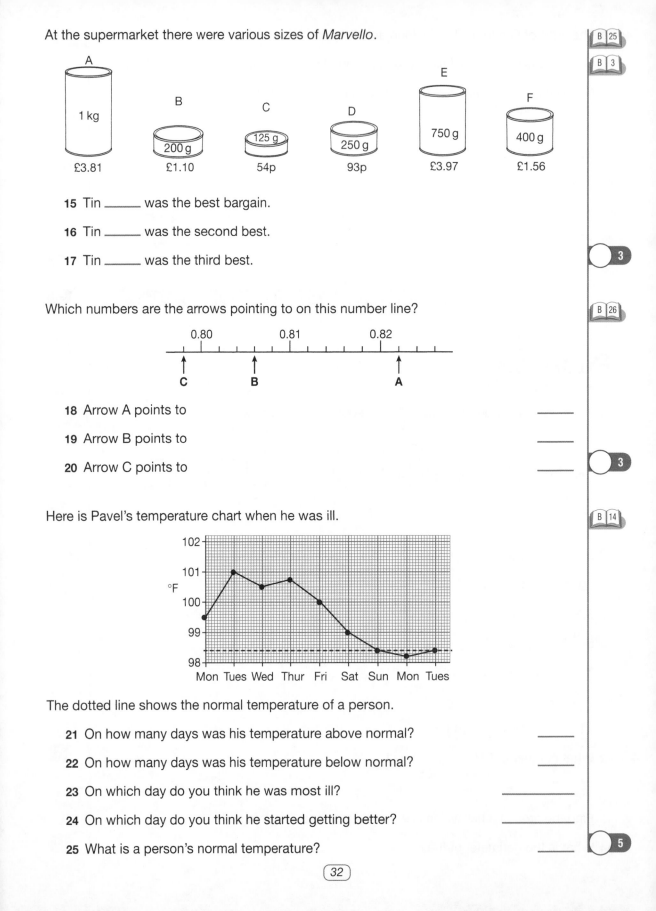

A	B	C	D	E	F
1 kg	200 g	125 g	250 g	750 g	400 g
£3.81	£1.10	54p	93p	£3.97	£1.56

15 Tin _____ was the best bargain.

16 Tin _____ was the second best.

17 Tin _____ was the third best.

Which numbers are the arrows pointing to on this number line?

0.80   0.81   0.82

C   B   A

18 Arrow A points to   _____

19 Arrow B points to   _____

20 Arrow C points to   _____

Here is Pavel's temperature chart when he was ill.

The dotted line shows the normal temperature of a person.

21 On how many days was his temperature above normal?   _____

22 On how many days was his temperature below normal?   _____

23 On which day do you think he was most ill?   _____

24 On which day do you think he started getting better?   _____

25 What is a person's normal temperature?   _____

B 25
B 3
3
B 26
3
B 14
5

In the end-of-term tests Zanna got the following marks.

Mathematics	$\frac{54}{75}$	English	$\frac{48}{60}$
History	$\frac{27}{40}$	French	$\frac{25}{40}$
Geography	$\frac{39}{50}$	Art	$\frac{15}{20}$

B 10

26 Her best subject was   _____

27 2nd was   _____

28 3rd was   _____

29 4th was   _____

30 5th was   _____

31 6th was   _____

◯ 6

Complete these sequences.

B 7

32–33	12	13	15	18	_____	_____
34–35	5000	500	50	5	_____	_____
36–37	$\frac{3}{4}$	1	$1\frac{1}{2}$	$2\frac{1}{2}$	_____	_____
38–39	0.6	0.7	0.8	0.9	_____	_____
40–41	0.125	0.25	0.375	0.5	_____	_____

B11 B10

◯ 10

Here are the scores in a mental arithmetic test out of 20.

B 15

Name	Peter	Cressida	Petra	Greg	Helen
Score	17	16	18	16	17

42–43 There are two modes: what are they?   _____   _____

44 What is the **median**?   _____

45 What is the **range**?   _____

46 What is the **mean**?   _____

Peter's test was wrongly marked and he should have got 16 not 17.

47 Which score is the **mode** now?   _____

48 What is the **median** now?   _____

49 What is the **range** now?   _____

50 What is the **mean** now?   _____

◯ 9

Now go to the Progress Chart to record your score!   Total ◯ 50

Paper 13

1–3 Complete the figures below. The dotted line is the line of symmetry.

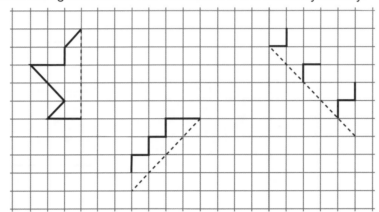

3

Underline the correct answer in each line.

4 $\frac{1}{5} + \frac{2}{10}$ $=$ $\frac{3}{15}$ $\frac{2}{5}$ $\frac{3}{10}$ $\frac{5}{10}$ $\frac{1}{5}$

5 $0.49 \div 7$ $=$ 7 0.7 0.07 70 700

6 20% of 35 $=$ 7 8 15 20 25

7 $4^2 - 3^2$ $=$ 1 2 3 7 9

8 $2^3 - 2^2$ $=$ 1 2 3 4 5

9 25% of 1 metre $=$ 1 cm 2 cm 10 cm 25 cm 25 m

10 $0.1 \times 0.1 \times 0.1 =$ 0.3 0.2 0.001 0.003 0.0001

11 $\frac{1}{3} + \frac{1}{6}$ $=$ $\frac{2}{3}$ $\frac{1}{2}$ $\frac{1}{9}$ $\frac{2}{9}$ $\frac{1}{18}$

8

12–14 Share £3.40 among Angela, Maya and Claire. For every 10p Angela gets, Maya gets 5p, and Claire gets 2p.

Angela gets _____, Maya gets _____ and Claire gets _____ .

3

15 $\frac{3}{4}$ of a sum of money is £1.80. What is $\frac{1}{3}$ of it? _____

16 Multiply 3.7 by itself, and then take 3.7 from the answer. _____

17 Add together 3.7, 2.95 and 0.187. _____

18 Take 1.689 from 3.2. _____

19 Divide 799 by 17. _____

5

Multiply each of the numbers below by 1000.

20 2.75 _____

21 38.2 _____

22 0.125 _____

23 0.875 _____

4

The bar chart below shows the marks in Mathematics for Class 8.

The maximum mark was 100.
One boy gained over 90.

$\frac{2}{5}$ of those who received between 81 and 90 were girls.

$\frac{3}{4}$ of those who received between 71 and 80 were boys.

$\frac{1}{2}$ of those who received between 61 and 70 were girls.

$\frac{1}{3}$ of those who received between 51 and 60 were girls.

$\frac{1}{2}$ of those who received between 41 and 50 were boys.

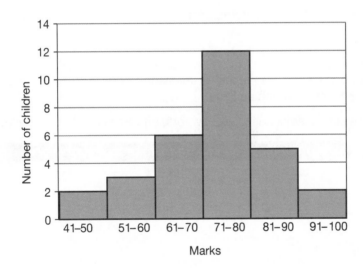

24 How many children took the test? _____

25 How many girls got over 90 marks? _____

26 How many boys received between 61 and 70 marks? _____

27 How many girls received between 41 and 50 marks? _____

28 In the 81 to 90 mark range, how many were boys? _____

29 In the 71 to 80 mark range, how many were girls? _____

30 How many boys received between 51 and 60 marks? _____

7

31–40 Fill in the multiplication table.

×				
	___	8	18	___
	___	12	___	___
	35	___	___	14
	___	___	___	2

Fill in the missing numbers.

41 $\dfrac{4}{5} = \dfrac{}{25}$

42 $\dfrac{7}{11} = \dfrac{}{121}$

43 $\dfrac{7}{8} = \dfrac{}{64}$

44 $\dfrac{2}{7} = \dfrac{}{42}$

45 $\dfrac{3}{4} = \dfrac{}{48}$

46 $\dfrac{7}{9} = \dfrac{}{63}$

47 If 13 items cost £1.56, what would 7 items cost? £ _____

48–50 Share 39 sweets among Penny, Ragini and Prue giving Penny 3 times as much as Ragini, and Ragini 3 times as much as Prue.

Penny has _____ sweets, Ragini has _____ sweets, and Prue has _____ sweets.

Now go to the Progress Chart to record your score!   **Total**   50

Paper 14

1–3 Complete this table.

60	144	72	___	120
5	12	___	11	___

4   0.38
    × 11

   _____

5   ___
   9)5.13

6   1030
   − 752

   _____

36

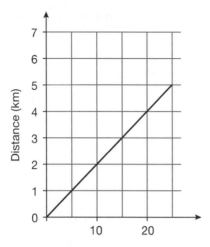

Distance (km) / Time (minutes)

Look at the line graph and then answer these questions.

7 I'll do 2 km in _____ minutes.

8 I'll do 1 km in _____ minutes.

9 How far will I travel in 25 minutes? _____

10 What is my speed in km/h? _____

11 What number, when multiplied by 25, gives the same answer as 45×40? _____

Solve these equations.

12 $3 + a = 15$
$a =$ _____

13 $x + 4 = 7$
$x =$ _____

14 $5 + a = 7$
$a =$ _____

15 $y - 7 = 9$
$y =$ _____

16 $b - 4 = 8$
$b =$ _____

17 $c - 1 = 5$
$c =$ _____

18–21 Do these divisions.

$7 \overline{)896}$ $6 \overline{)786}$ $9 \overline{)1188}$ $4 \overline{)516}$

22 Circle the division with the largest **quotient**.

It takes me 19 minutes to walk home from school.

23 If I leave school at 3:45 p.m. what time will I get home? _____

24 How many minutes are there from 10:29 p.m. on Monday to 2:05 a.m. on Tuesday? _____ minutes

37

Four schools in Sandville made these pie charts which show how many of their pupils walk to school.

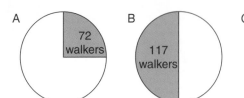 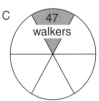 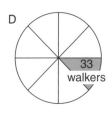

Write the total number of pupils in each school.

25 School A _____

26 School B _____

27 School C _____

28 School D _____

29 Angle x = _____

30 Angle $2x$ = _____

31 Angle a = _____

32 Angle b = _____

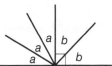

Complete the timetable below.

33–43 There are five 40-minute lessons, with a break of 15 minutes after the second lesson.

	Begins	**Ends**
1st lesson	_____	_____
2nd lesson	_____	_____
Break	_____	_____
3rd lesson	_____	_____
4th lesson	_____	_____
5th lesson	_____	12:50

44–45 There are 630 children in a school. There are 5 boys to every 4 girls.

There are _____ boys and _____ girls.

B 14
B 2
B 3
4
B 17
4
B 27
11
B 13
2

46–47 The perimeter of a rectangle is 40 cm. The length is 4 times the width.

The length is _____ cm and the width is _____ cm.

B 20

2

1 kg of *Britewash* costs £1.20. At this price per kg:

B 3

48 I could buy _____ with £6.00.

B 25

49 I could buy _____ with 30p.

50 I would have to pay _____ for 3.5 kg.

3

Now go to the Progress Chart to record your score! **Total** 50

Paper 15

Here are the scores in a Science test out of 50.

B 15

Name	Kamala	Matt	Rashid	Jo	James
Score	42	15	26	31	26

1 What is the **mode**? _____

2 What is the **median**? _____

3 What is the **range**? _____

4 What is the **mean**? _____

Matt actually got 25 not 15.

5 What is the median now? _____

6 What is the range now? _____

6

After I had bought a book costing £2.40, one third of what I had left was £1.20.

B4 B3

7 How much money did I have at first? _____

B 2

1

There are 24 children in our class. This Venn diagram shows how many of us belong to the Cycling Club (C) and how many of us belong to the Swimming Club (S).

B 14

B 2

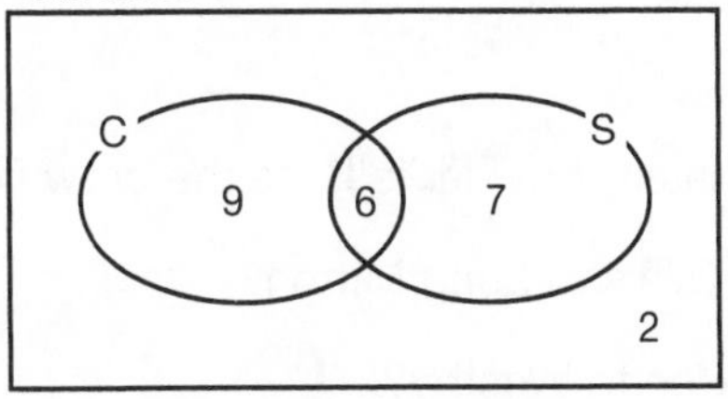

8 How many belong to the Cycling Club? _____

9 How many belong to the Swimming Club? _____

10 How many belong to both clubs ? _____

11 How many belong to neither club? _____

12 How many belong to one club only? _____

Our class

C 9 6 7 S

2

5

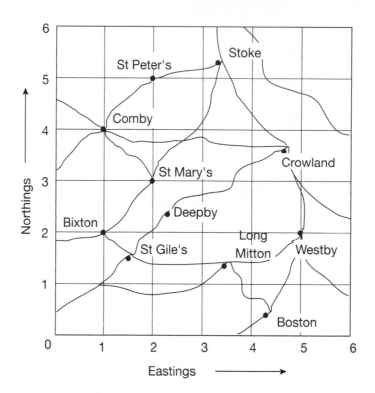

This map is covered with a grid, the lines of which are numbered 0−6 for eastings and 0−6 for northings. The position of towns is found by giving their **coordinates**, for example Bixton is (1, 2).

Some of the towns are not situated on the lines, but are inside the squares.

When this is so, the **coordinates** of the bottom left-hand corner of the square are given, for example Deepby is (2, 2).

Scale: A side of a small square represents 10 km.

Name the towns which are at the following positions.

13 (3, 1) _____

14 (4, 0) _____

Give the **coordinates** for the following towns.

15 Comby (_____ , _____)

16 Stoke (_____ , _____)

Approximately, how far is it, as the crow flies (in a straight line), from:

17 St Gile's to Long Mitton? _____

18 Bixton to Westby? _____

Your task is to guide the robot along the white squares on the plan.
It starts and finishes on one of the squares marked A, B, C, D or E.
It can only move FORWARD, turn RIGHT 90° and turn LEFT 90°.

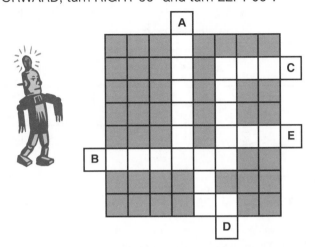

Complete these instructions to guide the robot along the white squares.

19 From A to B: FORWARD 6, RIGHT 90°, _____ .

20 From B to C: FORWARD 6, _____ , FORWARD 4, RIGHT 90°, FORWARD 3.

21 From C to E: FORWARD 3, LEFT 90°, _____ , LEFT 90°, FORWARD 3.

22–23 From D to B: FORWARD 1, LEFT 90°, FORWARD 1, _____ , _____ ,
LEFT 90°, FORWARD 5.

5

24–27 Jada used this decision tree to sort mobile phones. What is missing from the tree?
Fill in the gaps.

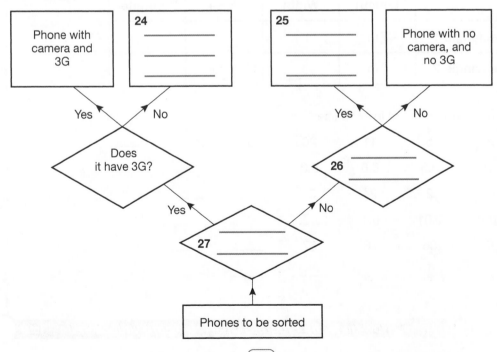

4

41

State whether the following statements are TRUE or FALSE.

28 Line B is parallel
to line C. _____

29 Line B is perpendicular
to line C. _____

30 Line B is a horizontal
line. _____

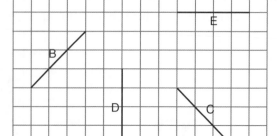

31 Put a circle around the **prime number**.

20   21   22   23   24   25

There are 364 children in a school. There are 18 more girls than boys.

32 There are _____ girls.

33 There are _____ boys.

34 Take eleven from eleven thousand.   _____

35–38 Complete the following table.

	Length	Width	Area	Perimeter
Rectangle 1	7 m	4 m	_____	_____
Rectangle 2	9 m	_____	36 m²	_____

Write the next two numbers in each line.

39–40 2   5   11   20   32   _____   _____

41–42 5.7   5.8   6.0   6.3   _____   _____

43–44 $1\frac{1}{2}$ 2 $2\frac{3}{4}$ $3\frac{3}{4}$ _____   _____

45–46 0.001   0.01   0.1   _____   _____

47–48 97   86   76   67   _____   _____

49–50 $\frac{1}{4}$ $\frac{3}{8}$ $\frac{1}{2}$ _____   _____

Paper 16

Here is a pie chart which shows how many computers pupils in Class 6C have at home.

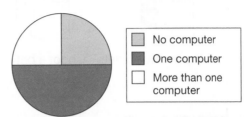

- No computer
- One computer
- More than one computer

1 What percentage of pupils have at least one computer at home? _____

2 What fraction of pupils have more than one computer at home? _____

If there are 32 pupils in Class 6C:

3 How many do not have a computer at home? _____

4 How many have at least one computer at home? _____

5 Find the smallest number which must be added to 890 to make it exactly divisible by 31. _____

6 Find the sum of 47, 48 and 49. _____

7 Find the **mean** of 47, 48 and 49. _____

8 Find the **range** of 47, 48 and 49. _____

Our school swimming pool, which is 50 m long and 20 m wide, has a path 10 m wide all around it.

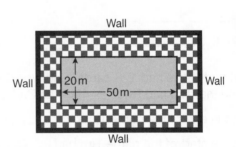

Wall

Wall   20 m   Wall
           ←50 m→

Wall

9 What is the area of the swimming pool? _____

10 What is the area of the whole complex (swimming pool and the path)? _____

11 What is the area of the path? _____

12 What is the perimeter of the swimming pool? _____

13 What is the total length of the wall? _____

14 Jenny bought 7 metres of material. She gave the assistant £20.00 and received £2.57 change.

What was the price of the material per metre? _____

Here are three shaded cubes.

 A   B   C

Which cube has the following nets? Choose between A, B, C or none.

15 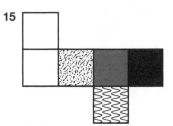 Is _____

16 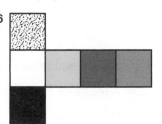 Is _____

17 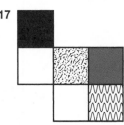 Is _____

18 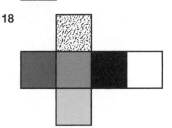 Is _____

What number is represented by the symbol in each equation?

19 $10 - ✳ = 27 \div 3$
✳ = _____

20 $3 + ✈ = 20 - 3$
✈ = _____

Divide each number by 1000.

21 34.2 _____

22 8.6 _____

23 274.6 _____

24 3 _____

Tim, Carl and Lewis had 126 cards. Carl won 3 from Tim, and Lewis lost 2 to Carl. They then found that Tim had twice as many as Carl, and Carl had twice as many as Lewis.

25–27 At the end of the game Tim had _____ , Carl had _____ and Lewis had _____ .

28–30 At the start of the game Tim had _____ , Carl had _____ and Lewis had _____ .

We asked 144 children at our school how they spent their holiday.
When we got their answers we made this pie chart.

31 How many children went to the beach? _____

32 How many went sailing? _____

33 The number of children who went on an Activity holiday was _____

34 How many went camping? _____

35 How many went canal boating? _____

In a school there were a total of 476 pupils and teachers.

The girls + the teachers = 241   The boys + the teachers = 258

36–38 There were _____ teachers, _____ boys and _____ girls.

Underline the correct answer in each line.

39 $\frac{1}{3} + \frac{1}{6}$ = $\frac{2}{3}$ $\frac{1}{2}$ $\frac{1}{9}$ $\frac{2}{9}$ $\frac{1}{6}$

40 $\frac{1}{5} + \frac{7}{10}$ = $\frac{8}{10}$ $\frac{8}{15}$ $\frac{9}{15}$ $\frac{11}{15}$ $\frac{9}{10}$

41 $111 - 19$ = 100   128   102   82   92

42 $6 \div 1.2$ = 48   5   50   0.5   5.3

43 $3^3 - 5^2$ = 8   15   3   2   1

44 $60 \div 3$ = 4   8   20   32   57

45 25% of 48 = 12   24   25   48   60

46 $\frac{1}{4} \times \frac{1}{4}$ = 1 $\frac{1}{8}$ $\frac{1}{16}$ $\frac{1}{2}$ $\frac{1}{6}$

47–48 Put a circle around the **prime numbers**.

13   14   15   16   17

49–50 Underline the **prime factors** of 18.

2   3   4   5   6   7   8

Now go to the Progress Chart to record your score!   Total   50

Paper 17

1–5 Here are Ajay's exam marks. Change them into percentages.

Subject	Actual mark	Possible mark	Percentage
Science	12	15	_____
French	21	35	_____
English	68	80	_____
Art	63	70	_____
Music	14	20	_____

6 Ajay's total mark in Science and French was _____ out of 50.

7 What is Ajay's total mark in Science and French expressed as a percentage? _____

8–12 Write down Peter's actual marks.

Subject	Actual mark	Possible mark	Percentage
Science	_____	15	60
French	_____	35	80
English	_____	80	55
Art	_____	70	70
Music	_____	20	65

13 Peter's total mark in English and Art was _____ out of 150.

14 What is Peter's total mark in English and Art expressed as a percentage? _____

Write each of these numbers to the nearest whole number.

15 8.35 _____   **16** 0.71 _____

17 4.48 _____   **18** 0.123 _____

19–21 There are 56 beads. Sam has twice as many as Ren, who has twice as many as Aisha.

Sam has _____ beads, Ren has _____ beads and Aisha has _____ beads.

These are the nets of solids. What solids will they make? Choose four from: square-based pyramid, triangular-based pyramid, triangular prism, pentagonal prism, cube, cuboid, sphere or cone.

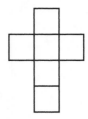 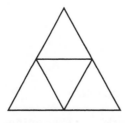 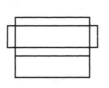 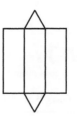

22 _____   **23** _____   **24** _____   **25** _____

26
```
   7946
   5878
   6575
 + 9876
 _____

 _____
```

27 Write the answer to the last calculation in words. _____

_____

28–37 Complete the following chart.

	Length	Width	Perimeter	Area
Rectangle 1	29 m	_____	60 m	_____
Rectangle 2	28 m	_____	60 m	_____
Rectangle 3	_____	5 m	60 m	_____
Rectangle 4	_____	10 m	60 m	_____
Rectangle 5	15 m	_____	60 m	_____

10

38 Multiply 0.0908 by 25. _____

B 11

1

39–41 Convert this recipe for pasta from imperial to metric units (to the nearest 5 g).

Use the approximation: 1 oz = 25 g

B 25

Ingredient	Imperial	Metric
Plain flour	5 oz	_____
Semolina flour	12 oz	_____
Eggs	11 eggs	_____

3

Give the most appropriate metric unit to measure:

B 25

42 the distance from Earth to the Sun. _____ **43** the amount of petrol in a car. _____

44 the weight of a train. _____ **45** the thickness of this book. _____

4

46–50 Put these numbers in order, smallest first. 0.707 0.78 0.708 0.7 0.77

B 1

_____ _____ _____ _____ _____

5

Now go to the Progress Chart to record your score! **Total** 50

Paper 18

1 In a class, 19 children have dogs and 18 children have cats.

If 15 children have both dogs and cats, find the smallest possible number of children in the class. _____

B4 B2

2 How many times can 27 be subtracted from 1431? _____

B3 B2

3 Twelve toys were bought for £1.25 each and sold for £1.60 each.

What was the total profit? _____

B4 B3

B 2

3

4–15 Here are some exchange rates.

£1 = 1.14 US dollars
£1 = 93.2 Indian rupee
£1 = 1.12 euros
£1 = 1.58 Canadian dollars

Complete the table.

£	US dollars	Indian rupee	Euros	Canadian dollars
£10.00	_____	_____	_____	_____
£5.00	_____	_____	_____	_____
£0.50	_____	_____	_____	_____

16–19 Arrange these numbers in order, putting the largest first.

7.8   7.088   7.88   7.008   _____   _____   _____   _____

20–25 Complete the following table.

Fraction	Decimal	Percentage
$\frac{1}{2}$	_____	_____
_____	0.25	_____
$\frac{1}{5}$	_____	_____

26–30 Solve these equations.

$$\frac{56}{a} = 8 \qquad \frac{49}{b} = 7 \qquad \frac{72}{9} = x \qquad \frac{y}{4} = 3 \qquad \frac{z}{9} = 7$$

$a =$ _____ $b =$ _____ $x =$ _____ $y =$ _____ $z =$ _____

31 The product of two numbers is 111.

The larger number is 37. What is the other number?   _____

What are the missing numbers in these number squares?

49	36	25
36	25	16
25	16	x

y	30.2	25.8
30.2	25.8	21.4
25.8	21.4	17

$\frac{1}{2}$	$\frac{5}{8}$	$\frac{3}{4}$
$\frac{3}{8}$	$\frac{1}{2}$	$\frac{5}{8}$
z	$\frac{3}{8}$	$\frac{1}{2}$

32 $x =$ _____   **33** $y =$ _____   **34** $z =$ _____

	Train A	Train B	Train C	Train D
Westbury	08:11	09:20	18:09 ↑	20:09 ↑
Trowbridge	08:19	09:30	17:58	20:04
Bath	08:45	09:54	17:23	19:31
Bristol	↓ 09:00	↓ 10:11	17:05	19:17

35 How long does the slowest train take to do the entire journey? _____

36 If I live in Westbury, and want to be in Bath before 9 a.m., on which train must I travel? _____

37 How long does the 19:31 from Bath take to travel to Westbury? _____

38 When should the 17:23 from Bath arrive in Westbury? _____

4

Using this world time chart answer the following questions.

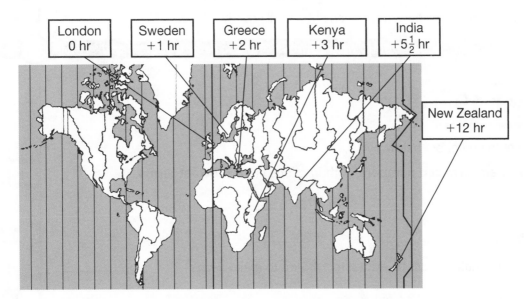

London 0 hr   Sweden +1 hr   Greece +2 hr   Kenya +3 hr   India +5½ hr

New Zealand +12 hr

39 When it is 10:00 a.m. in London, what time is it in New Zealand? _____

40 When it is 9:00 a.m. in London, what time is it in India? _____

41 When it is 3:30 p.m. in Greece, what time is it in London? _____

42 When it is 1:15 p.m. in Sweden, what time is it in London? _____

43 If I made a telephone call from Kenya to India at 3:00 p.m., what time would it be in India? _____

5

	Years	Months
Tony is	10	8
Claire is	9	6
Abdel is	11	4
Mandy is	10	2

44 Look at the table. The children's ages add up to _____ years _____ months

45–46 What is the **mean** age of the four children? _____ years _____ months

B 2
B 15

3

Here is a box 20 cm long, 10 cm wide, and 8 cm high.

A ribbon is placed round the box, once lengthwise, and once round the width.

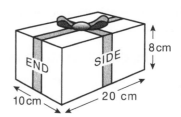

47 What is the perimeter of the side of the box? _____

48 What is the perimeter of the end of the box? _____

49 What is the perimeter of the base of the box? _____

50 If I allow 35 cm for the bow, how much ribbon will I need? _____

B 20
B 2

4

Now go to the Progress Chart to record your score! **Total** 50

Paper 19

Divide each of the numbers below by 10.

Give your answers as **mixed numbers**, with fractions in their **lowest terms**.

1 78 _____   **2** 475 _____

3 312.5 _____   **4** 1.25 _____

5 How many metres must be added to 1.35 km to make 4 km? _____

B 3
B 10

4

B 25

1

B 3

6–13 Fill in the multiplication grid.

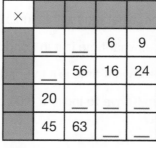

×			6	9
	__	__	6	9
	__	56	16	24
	20	__	__	__
	45	63	__	__

8

Write each of these values in decimal form.

14 17 tenths _____   **15** 143 hundredths _____

16 47 units _____   **17** 7 thousandths _____

18 259 tens _____   **19** 14 hundredths _____

Insert signs to make the following correct.

20–22 5 _____ 5 _____ 1 = 13 _____ 12

23–25 (3 _____ 2) _____ 5 = 50 _____ 2

Insert the missing numbers in these calculations.

26 $4.9 \times$ _____ $= 490$

27 _____ $\div 10 = 0.123$

28 $0.136 \times 100 =$ _____

29 The average of 6 numbers is 4.

If one of the numbers is 2, what is the average of the other 5 numbers?   _____

30–35 VAT (Value Added Tax) is added to the price of some goods.
It is charged at 20% (£20.00 on each £100).
Complete the following table.

Price before VAT	VAT	Total price
£530	_____	_____
£165	_____	_____
£62	_____	_____

36–41 Three rectangular pieces of card have the same area (24 cm²).
Fill in the other measurements.

	Length	Width	Perimeter	Area
Piece A	8 cm	_____ cm	_____ cm	24 cm²
Piece B	_____ cm	4 cm	_____ cm	24 cm²
Piece C	12 cm	_____ cm	_____ cm	24 cm²

What percentages are the following fractions?

42 $\frac{15}{30} =$ _____   **43** $\frac{4}{25} =$ _____

Look at the diagram. Answer the questions below by writing YES or NO.

It would help you if you drew in the diagonals with a ruler.

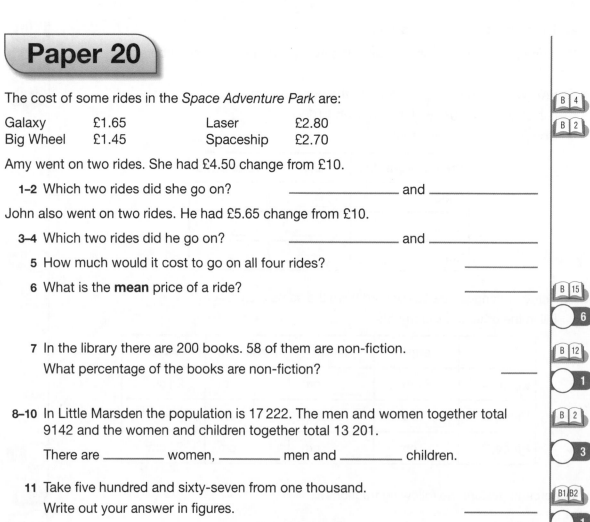

B 17
B 19

44 Are all the sides the same length? _____

45 Are the opposite sides parallel? _____

46 Are all the angles equal? _____

47 Are the diagonals the same length? _____

48 Do the diagonals cross at right angles? _____

49 Is this a **rhombus**? _____

50 Is this a **parallelogram**? _____

7

Now go to the Progress Chart to record your score!   Total   50

Paper 20

The cost of some rides in the *Space Adventure Park* are:

| Galaxy | £1.65 | Laser | £2.80 |
| Big Wheel | £1.45 | Spaceship | £2.70 |

B 4
B 2

Amy went on two rides. She had £4.50 change from £10.

1–2 Which two rides did she go on? _____ and _____

John also went on two rides. He had £5.65 change from £10.

3–4 Which two rides did he go on? _____ and _____

5 How much would it cost to go on all four rides? _____

6 What is the **mean** price of a ride? _____

B 15

6

7 In the library there are 200 books. 58 of them are non-fiction.

What percentage of the books are non-fiction? _____

B 12

1

8–10 In Little Marsden the population is 17 222. The men and women together total 9142 and the women and children together total 13 201.

There are _____ women, _____ men and _____ children.

B 2

3

11 Take five hundred and sixty-seven from one thousand.
Write out your answer in figures. _____

B1 B2

1

Complete the figures below. The dotted line is the line of symmetry.

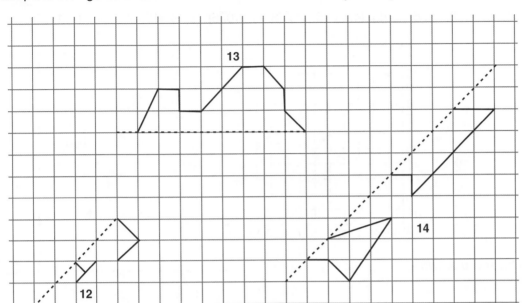

B 24

3

The big hand of a clock is at 12 and the small hand is not. If the little hand moves in a clockwise direction, what time is it when the angle between the two hands is:

B 27
B 17

15 180°? ——— o'clock

16 30°? ——— o'clock

17 120°? ——— o'clock

18 60°? ——— o'clock

19 150°? ——— o'clock

20 90°? ——— o'clock

6

21 John multiplied a number by 9 instead of dividing it by 9.

His answer was 4131. What should his answer have been? ———

B 3

22 20% of my money is £2.55.

What is $\frac{2}{5}$ of it? ———

B12 B10

23 What amount must be added to 178.5 g to make 1 kg? ——— g

B 25

3

Circle the correct answers in each line.

B3 B6

24 13 × 11 = 132 143 133

25 15^2 = 165 155 225

26 64 = 8^2 9^2 7^2

27 702 ÷ 3 = 214 234 204

28 14 × 12 = 154 148 168

5

Plot these points and join them in order.

29–41 (5, 1) (5, 5) (2, 3) (5, 6) (2, 5) (4, 7) (6, 11) (8, 7) (10, 5) (7, 6) (10, 3) (7, 5) (7, 1)

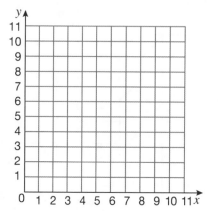

42 What have you drawn? _____ 14

The three largest oceans in the world cover the following areas.

Ocean	Square km	Square miles
Atlantic	82 217 000	31 736 000
Indian	73 481 000	28 364 000
Pacific	165 384 000	63 838 000

Write the answers to the following questions in the table below.

43–44 Round the areas of the Atlantic Ocean to the nearest 100 000.

45–46 Round the areas of the Indian Ocean to the nearest 10 000.

47–48 Round the areas of the Pacific Ocean to the nearest 1 000 000.

Ocean	Square km	Square miles
Atlantic	_____	_____
Indian	_____	_____
Pacific	_____	_____

6

Last Friday $\frac{1}{8}$ of the pupils in our school were absent.
There are 560 pupils altogether in the school.

49–50 There were _____ pupils absent and _____ pupils present.

2

Now go to the Progress Chart to record your score! Total 50

54

Paper 21

The products of the following calculations are either odd or even. Answer each question as either ODD or EVEN.

B 3

1 84 × 36 is an _____ number.

2 163 × 297 is an _____ number.

3 729 × 1468 is an _____ number.

4 292 × 36 × 52 is an _____ number.

4

Write the following amounts correct to the nearest £1.00.

B 1

5 £2.42 _____   **6** £2.71 _____   **7** £4.59 _____

8 £6.49 _____   **9** £7.50 _____

5

$\frac{2}{3}$ of a sum of money is 48p.

B 10

10 What is $\frac{5}{8}$ of the sum of money?   _____

1

Roast chicken must be cooked for 50 minutes per kg and then for an extra 20 minutes.

B 3

11–16 Complete this table of cooking times in hours and minutes.

Weight of chicken (kg)	Cooking time
1	_____ h _____ min
1.5	_____ h _____ min
2	_____ h _____ min
2.5	_____ h _____ min
3	_____ h _____ min
3.5	_____ h _____ min

6

Divide these numbers by 1000.

B 1

17 374 _____   **18** 14.8 _____   **19** 2.55 _____

3

There are 420 children in a school. 45% of the pupils are boys.

B 12

20 How many boys are there?   _____

21 How many girls are there?   _____

2

£9.00 is shared between Amanda, Anita and Claire in the ratio of 8:5:2.

B 13

22 Amanda receives _____ .   **23** Anita receives _____ .   **24** Claire receives _____ .

3

25–29 Arrange these fractions in order, largest first.

$$\frac{7}{12} \qquad \frac{3}{8} \qquad \frac{3}{4} \qquad \frac{11}{24} \qquad \frac{5}{6}$$

_____ _____ _____ _____

B 10
5

Suggest the best imperial unit to measure:

30 the distance from London to New York.

31 the amount of water in a jug.

32 the weight of a pencil.

33 the height of a man.

_____

_____

_____

_____

B 25
4

Convert these 24-hour clock times into 12-hour clock times.

| 20:20 | 08:05 | 00:10 | 17:45 |

32 _____   **35** _____   **36** _____   **37** _____

B 27
4

38–39 Add these children's ages.

	Years	Months
Zoe	10	11
Simon	10	8
David	11	4
Rachel	10	2
Tariq	10	8
Total	_____	_____

B 2
B 15

40–41 What is their average age?   _____ years _____ months

4

Add the greatest value to the smallest.

42 $£\frac{1}{2}$ £0.55 $27 \times 2p$ $£\frac{13}{25}$ £1.00 − 49p   _____

B10/B3
B 2
1

Scott has $\frac{1}{3}$ as many computer games as Anish, and Anish has $\frac{1}{2}$ as many games as Nick.

Together they have 140 games. How many do they have each?

43 Scott has _____ games.   **44** Anish has _____ games.   **45** Nick has _____ games.

B 10
B 13
3

We asked 72 children to name their favourite colour.
We made this pie chart.

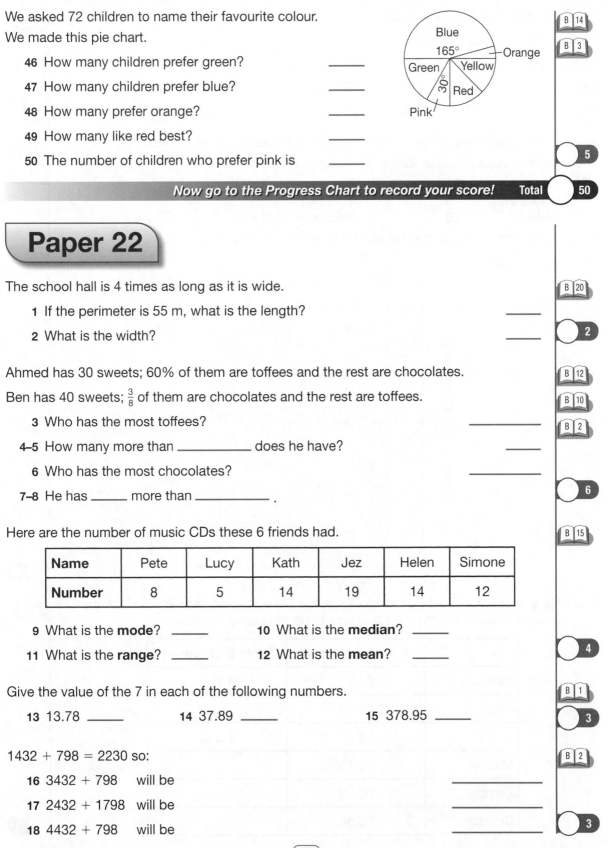

46 How many children prefer green? _____

47 How many children prefer blue? _____

48 How many prefer orange? _____

49 How many like red best? _____

50 The number of children who prefer pink is _____

Now go to the Progress Chart to record your score!   Total   50

Paper 22

The school hall is 4 times as long as it is wide.

1 If the perimeter is 55 m, what is the length? _____

2 What is the width? _____

Ahmed has 30 sweets; 60% of them are toffees and the rest are chocolates.

Ben has 40 sweets; $\frac{3}{8}$ of them are chocolates and the rest are toffees.

3 Who has the most toffees? _____

4–5 How many more than _____ does he have? _____

6 Who has the most chocolates? _____

7–8 He has _____ more than _____ .

Here are the number of music CDs these 6 friends had.

Name	Pete	Lucy	Kath	Jez	Helen	Simone
Number	8	5	14	19	14	12

9 What is the **mode**? _____   10 What is the **median**? _____

11 What is the **range**? _____   12 What is the **mean**? _____

Give the value of the 7 in each of the following numbers.

13 13.78 _____   14 37.89 _____   15 378.95 _____

1432 + 798 = 2230 so:

16 3432 + 798   will be   _____

17 2432 + 1798   will be   _____

18 4432 + 798   will be   _____

57

Fill in the next two numbers in each line.

19–20 95   89   84   80   _____   _____

21–22 89   77   67   59   _____   _____

23–24 31   33   36   40   _____   _____

25–26 144   121   100   81   _____   _____

27–32 On the grid below, draw a bar chart to show the following information.
The number of cups of coffee sold at Buttercup Café last week:

Monday	90	Tuesday	110
Wednesday	70	Thursday	100
Friday	120	Saturday	140

Be careful to use a scale that will show this information accurately.

Write in your scale.

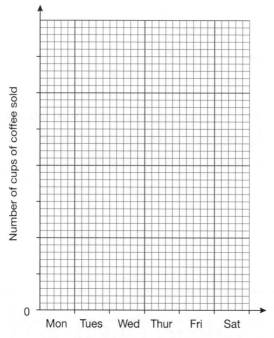

33–37 Here is part of a railway timetable. Fill in the times at which train B will reach the stations. It takes exactly the same time to do the journey as train A.

	Train A arrives at	Train B arrives at
Barwich	07:30	10:05
Hoole	07.48	_____
Carby	08.02	_____
Manton	08.15	_____
Pemby	08.29	_____
Durwich	08.54	_____

Your task is to guide the robot along the white squares on the plan.

It starts and finishes on one of the squares marked A, B, C, D or E.

It can only move FORWARD, turn RIGHT 90° and turn LEFT 90°.

Complete these instructions to guide the robot along the white squares.

38–39 From A to B: FORWARD 2, _____ , FORWARD 1, RIGHT 90°, FORWARD 3, LEFT 90°, _____ , RIGHT 90°, FORWARD 4

40–41 From B to C: FORWARD 4, LEFT 90°, FORWARD 1, RIGHT 90°, _____ , LEFT 90°, FORWARD 3, _____ , FORWARD 1, RIGHT 90°, FORWARD 2

42–43 From C to D: FORWARD 2, LEFT 90°, FORWARD 1, RIGHT 90°, FORWARD 3, LEFT 90°, FORWARD 1, _____ , _____ , LEFT 90°, FORWARD 1, RIGHT 90°, FORWARD 2

44 A coil of rope was divided into 7 equal sections, each 17.5 metres long. If there were 3.25 m left, how long was the rope?   _____

45 How many days were there between the 4th January and the 2nd March 2007? Do not include either of the given dates.   _____

46 A greenhouse can be bought by paying a deposit of £45, and then 12 monthly payments of £37.50.

What would be the total cost of the greenhouse?   _____

47 How many fifths are there in $12\frac{4}{5}$?   _____

48 What is the smallest number into which 6, 8, 10 and 12 will all divide without remainder?   _____

49 The houses on Union Street are all on one side, and are numbered 1, 2, 3, 4 and so on.

If the house with the middle number is number 37, how many houses are there in the street?   _____

50 Scarcroft United had 5000 spectators to watch their game this week. Each stand seats 870. What is the fewest number of stands required for this crowd?   _____

1–10 Complete this multiplication table.

×				
	___	___	48	___
	___	___	30	___
	11	9	___	___
	66	___	___	24

  10

Write the numbers below correct to the nearest 100.

  4

11 71 246 _____   **12** 1486 _____

13 1274 _____   **14** 704.85 _____

15 What number is halfway between 98 and 144? _____

  1

16–18 At Black Horse Junior School there were altogether 394 teachers and children.

The teachers and the boys numbered 189, and the girls and teachers together numbered 217.

There were _____ teachers, _____ boys and _____ girls.

  3

19 Make 478 three hundred times as large. _____

  1

20–23 Complete this table.

✤ = a + 3

  4

a	___	1	___	3
✤	3	___	5	___

Look in the circle and find the answers to these questions.

24 $9^2 - 8^2 =$ _____   **25** $11^2 - 9^2 =$ _____

26 $2^3 + 2^2 =$ _____   **27** $5^2 - 4^2 =$ _____

20 8
18 41
9
12 16 17
40

  4

Find the area of these triangles. Scale: 1 square = 1 cm²

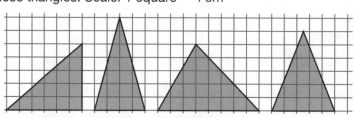

28 _____   **29** _____   **30** _____   **31** _____ 4

Divide the year 2007 into 2 parts so that the second part is 4 times as large as the first part.

B 13

32 How many days are there in the shorter part? _____

B 27

33 In the larger part there are _____ days.

34 If the shorter part starts on January 1st, when does it end? _____

3

35 If $\frac{5}{12}$ of the contents of a box weigh 20 kg, what is the weight of all the contents? _____

B 10

36 What would $\frac{1}{8}$ of the contents weigh? _____

2

37–40 Fill in the missing numbers.

a	2	35	_____	47	_____
3a	6	_____	231	_____	267

B 3

4

41 By how much is the product of 27 and 13 greater than their sum? _____

B3 B2

1

There are 180 sheep in a flock. For every 9 white sheep there is 1 black sheep. How many:

B 13

42 white sheep are there? _____   **43** black sheep are there? _____

2

Mr Pin paid £7.05 for 1.5 metres of material.

B 3

44 What was the cost per metre? _____

45 How much would 3.5 m cost? _____

2

46 What is the next odd number after 160 into which 9 will divide without remainder? _____

B3 B5

1

47–50 Write these fractions in decimal form.

$3\frac{1}{8}$ $4\frac{1}{20}$ $7\frac{5}{8}$ $9\frac{3}{40}$ _____ _____ _____ _____

B 10

4

Now go to the Progress Chart to record your score!   **Total**   50

Paper 24

Underline the correct answer in each line.

B 10

B 11

1 $\frac{1}{3} + \frac{1}{4}$ $=$ $\frac{1}{7}$ $\frac{7}{12}$ $\frac{2}{7}$ $\frac{2}{12}$

2 $10 - 1.99$ $=$ 9.11   8.01   11.99   9.01

3 0.04×0.4 $=$ 0.016   0.16   0.08   0.0016

4 4 ÷ 0.02   =   20   2   0.2   200

5 17.89 ÷ 10 =   178.9   1789   1.789   17.89

6 2.7 × 200   =   5.4   540   54.0   0.54

7 The perimeter of a square is 28 cm. What is its area?   _____

8   147
       × 49

       _____

9–15 On the grid below draw a bar chart to show the information in the table.
Be careful to use a scale which will show this information accurately.
Write in your scale.

Shop	Cameras sold
A	225
B	75
C	150
D	175
E	300
F	125
G	200

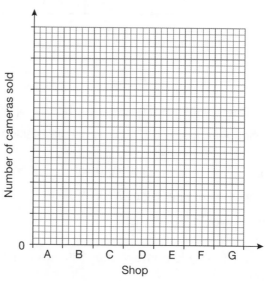

16 How many tiles, each 50 cm × 50 cm, would be needed to cover a floor
5 metres × 4 metres?   _____

17 What would be the cost of these tiles if I had to pay £7.50 for 10 tiles?   _____

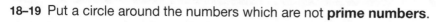

18–19 Put a circle around the numbers which are not **prime numbers**.

3   13   23   33   43   53   63

20–23 What are the **factors** of 21?   _____ , _____ , _____ , _____

24–25 Underline the **prime factors** of 21.

2   3   4   5   6   7   8

26 How many times can 34 be subtracted from 986?   _____

Ted has £98 and Zac has £64.

27 How much must Ted give to Zac so that they each have the same amount? _____

B2/B3

28 Would you estimate the number of children in a class to the nearest 10, 100, 1000? _____

29 Would you estimate the number of people at a Premier League football game to the nearest 10, 1000, 10 000 or 1 000 000? _____

30 The area of the flag is _____.

31 The area of the cross is _____.

32 The shaded part has an area of _____.

33 The perimeter of the flag is _____.

34 The perimeter of the cross is _____.

35–42 Complete the following table.

Fraction	Decimal	Percentage
$\frac{3}{10}$	_____	_____
$\frac{7}{100}$	_____	_____
_____	0.25	_____
$\frac{1}{20}$	_____	_____

43 $8 - 1.127 =$ _____   44 $47.625 \div 2.5 =$ _____

45–50 Complete the following table.

Wholesale price	Retail price	Profit
£18.75	£23.50	_____
_____	£70.20	£11.35
£5.13	_____	97p
£196.50	£235.25	_____
_____	£13.50	£2.19
93p	_____	19p

Now go to the Progress Chart to record your score!   Total   50

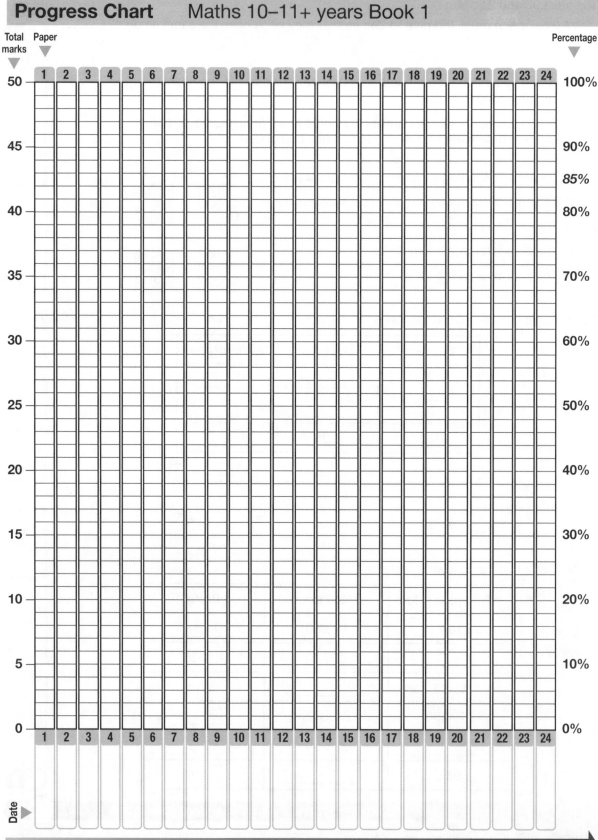

Progress Chart   Maths 10–11+ years Book 1

Total marks

Paper

Percentage

	1	2	3	4	5	6	7	8	9	10	11	12	13	14	15	16	17	18	19	20	21	22	23	24	

50 — 100%

45 — 90%
— 85%

40 — 80%

35 — 70%

30 — 60%

25 — 50%

20 — 40%

15 — 30%

10 — 20%

5 — 10%

0 — 0%

Date

When you've finished the book use the Next Steps Planner →